S0-BVP-294

Crisis: The Loss of Europe

Other Books by Charles A. Cerami

Successful Leadership in Business

How to Solve Management Problems

Living the Business Life

Alliance Born of Danger

Charles A. Cerami

Crisis: The Loss of Europe

Harcourt Brace Jovanovich
New York and London

Printed in the United States of America

Library of Congress Cataloging in Publication Data

Cerami, Charles A
Crisis, the loss of Europe.

Includes index.
1. European Economic Community. 2. European Economic Community—United States. I. Title.
HC241.2.C42 341.24'2 74-20936
ISBN 0-15-123097-8

First edition

BCDE

To Lisa, with love:

from the title

to the last word

Contents

Crisis: The Loss of Europe

1

The Reason Why

One afternoon in 1965 Assistant Secretary of State James L. Greenfield, who had just returned from a weekend session at President Johnson's Texas ranch, startled me with these words of advice: "Don't make the mistake of writing that the US will ease out of Vietnam. You'll be much closer to right if you assume an even bigger American build-up there." South Vietnam was in danger of collapse at that moment. The communist forces were threatening Saigon itself. America's President faced the dreadful decision between abandoning the rescue effort that Eisenhower and Kennedy had begun or pouring in enough new forces to make it Washington's own war against the combined efforts of North Vietnam, China, and Russia.

"President Johnson has always thought of Dean Acheson as the man who lost China," Greenfield confided. "And he is absolutely determined not to be the man who loses the rest of Asia. After all the hours I've just spent with him I can assure you that whatever the cost, we'll stay there."

The cost was . . . Europe.

Not until the next millennium will it be possible to analyze the wisdom of this trade. America's stand in Vietnam interrupted communism's advance in Southeast Asia and Indonesia, caused huge tremors within China, and thereby altered relationships among all the major powers.

4
Crisis: The Loss of Europe

Historians of the future—depending on who rules that future—may even point back to this as a salutary moment. But the analyst of the coming decade can find only an unrewarded sacrifice. In order to fight communism in Asia, America gave up much of its power over Europe. American security was subtly jeopardized and US investments were more immediately menaced. The disunity that was soon to bring on a traumatic energy crisis began to grip the entire modern world. If this seems too strong, consider how things stood up to that point and how they stand today.

For twenty years after World War II America was supreme in Western Europe. Its people depended on Washington for their security and their prosperity, and they knew it. It was clear to all Europeans—even to those who resisted too much Americanization—that the US was the defender and the Soviet Union was the menace. Yet America made little use of its overwhelming power. Such disputes as there might be—over the export of chickens, carpets, or glass—were negotiated as business between equals. Washington might threaten trade retaliation, but never referred to its overall force. This restraint created still more gratitude in the minds of most European statesmen. Even in the midst of a disagreement, few of them doubted that they were part of a family whose differences would be resolved and whose head was basically reliable.

The European Community itself had been Washington's idea. More than a decade before the Treaty of Rome—the agreement signed in 1957 that officially created the EEC—a 1944 Library of Congress report on the postwar treatment of Germany urged a European federation as the only way to treat Germans as equals and yet keep them subject to restrictions. Later the US Congress wrote into the Marshall Plan law a stipulation that Europe must develop "a single large market such as we have in the United States." And an internal memorandum prepared in the US foreign aid agency in 1949 presaged the eventual European Common Market. It blamed the small European economies for the "lifeless and moribund character of contemporary Western European capitalism." As a cure, it called for ". . . the formation of a single pervasive and highly competitive domestic market in Western Europe of sufficient size and scope to support mass production for mass consumption."

This American feeling continued generally unshaken for the first dozen years of the Community's life. There were some slight misgivings about the growth of an economic giant when Britain was negotiating to enter the European Economic Community in the early 1960's. But the specter of how great a competitor that "single large market" might become was greatly overshadowed by the critical need to keep hyperactive Germany locked inside a larger unit. Moreover, the happy vision of a Europe that got along internally and that served as a strong bulwark against Russian aggression looked like one of the firmest building blocks of future American policy.

Even when three successive American Presidents—Eisenhower, Kennedy, and Johnson—tended to take Europe for granted, they only slowed the momentum of Atlantic relations momentarily, because America's supremacy and America's integrity were unimpaired. But the raising of Vietnam to the status of a major war, against all the wishes and counseling of the European allies, stopped that momentum completely. And nothing—logical or emotional—is in sight that seems capable of restarting it.

Although Henry Kissinger, both as a White House aide and as Secretary of State, made a number of public pronouncements about revitalizing the US-European relationship, these rang hollowly. They were not based on practical economics or politics. Indeed, some of the men close to him believe that Kissinger is aligned with—or has inspired—a faction that hopes to divide and weaken Europe in order to clear away an irritant to American global policies. Time and again, especially in late 1973 and throughout 1974, his calls for conferences or joint actions seemed designed to spotlight the differences within Europe. While I think it likely that Kissinger is merely reacting to harsh reality as he sees it, rather than setting out to create discord, it is a sorry thing to find the facts of Atlantic life so much altered.

Vietnam first soured Europe psychologically, for America proclaimed itself not only world policeman, but world judge as well. This is no airy exaggeration. In the early part of his Administration, President Lyndon Johnson instructed some of our diplomats to let foreign governments know that we would continue our Vietnam fight even if every other country in the world were against us. At another time, when I told a top cabinet official at lunch that Europeans felt we didn't care about their opinions on our Asian policy, he tried to make sure that I would convey his sentiments by saying, "That's exactly right. You can tell them for me that we don't give a good goddamn what they think. We are carrying the whole burden, and their cheap criticism means nothing to us."

But beyond psychology, the Vietnam War created a more tangible barrier between the US and Europe: a mountain of depreciating dollars. Vietnam sickened the US economy and balance of payments. Our attempt to fight a sizable war without price controls or rationing or belt-tightening of any kind tripled the US rate of inflation and made our products less competitive abroad. This hampered our overseas sales and encouraged abnormally high imports, thus causing billions of American dollars to flow into European hands. All this wealth that first delighted the Europeans began to appall them as they realized that American paper money was losing its value or its buying power at the rate of six per cent or more per year. While a European businessman or hotelkeeper might still welcome the cash, more thoughtful or more informed Europeans began to feel that they were giving the US real goods and assets in return for dubious promissory notes. Especially painful was the fact that American companies had bought up tens of billions of dollars' worth of European factories with the questionable greenbacks.

So much for the European argument that the US forced Europe to give away some of its most desirable assets to finance a war that it detested, and then repudiated its obligations, declaring that it would no longer convert those paper dollars into gold or any other freely spendable asset. Like any family feud, this one has bitterness on the other side as well.

As seen from Washington, Europeans took only a few years to forget that their new prosperity was directly owed to the US. Not only did it start with Marshall Plan grants, loans, and technical help; America had also been one of Europe's great customers. It had eagerly and voluntarily cut its tariffs and tried to redistribute wealth when all the chips were on its side of the table. And those US factories in Europe had brought modern technology to the whole continent. Now Europe, fat and satisfied with its new prosperity, would not give an inch on trade. And it wanted no part of any other people's struggle for freedom. That was true not only of distant Vietnam; it was almost equally true of Europe's near neighbor, the Middle East. There, too, America had to bear the whole burden for defending Israel, while a number of European nations thought mainly about their oil needs or Mediterranean ambitions and made sure not to offend the Arabs.

For the sake of accuracy, it must be reported that many

observers on either side of the ocean tended to favor the *other* side's viewpoint. It goes without saying that many Americans viewed the Vietnam War much as the Europeans did, while some conservative Americans shared Europe's misgivings about the American dollar. On the other hand, not a few Europeans were dismayed by their countrymen's lack of interest in other parts of the world. "Please don't talk to me about the condition of Europe," a distinguished ambassador said to me across a table one night. "You will spoil my dinner. My countrymen and most others just want to close the doors and be merry, without thinking about the realities outside."

Whatever those realities outside might be, the blunt truth was that the economic effects of the Vietnam War brought America and Europe into confrontation. It is a tribute to the restraint of these continents that it did not immediately become a head-on clash. But beneath the public politeness there was serious trouble, even before today's differences over Mideast oil. Now the cracks are widening into fissures. When America's President calls for Atlantic unity, leaders in Britain, Germany, and France respond with polite words, but to insiders in the White House and in foreign capitals these are more form than substance. They know that self-preservation is growing as the chief thought in each nation's mind. And they know that some powerful men in Washington do have the secret and guilty wish that America's own brainchild—the European Economic Community—should be beset with enough internal divisions to leave our economy and our foreign policy free to go its own way. That the grandeur of the US postwar policy and the Atlantic Alliance should have descended to this is a great tragedy—and a great triumph for the quiet men in the Kremlin.

2

Brilliant Beginning

Rivalry will be the rule for the rest of the 1970's. The only question is how much order can be kept among the rivals on both sides of the ocean. To understand what is coming for Europe and how it will deal with America, look back for a moment at the start of this attempt to make it into one nation.

It began with a spirit of happy and willing sacrifice—with Germans, Italians, Belgians, Dutch of all ages saying, "We have had enough of national pride and petty conflicts. We want to be brothers."

This meant that drastic concessions would be required. And they were made.

Responding to the American encouragement of the late 1940's, many European statesmen began to work toward unity. There were innumerable meetings, mostly informal. Some—in the tradition of the European salon—were little more than social gatherings where carefully chosen guests turned the talk to serious subjects. Gradually, men who found their thinking to be along similar lines formed committees and action groups. They worked up reports and proposals, and they began to urge that more formal conferences be held.

A few names will help to give an idea of the sort of men who were the architects and builders of the project. Although he did not live to see his own country take part in the movement, Winston S. Churchill should be mentioned first, for—as on so many other subjects—he was well ahead of his time in speaking for a United States of Europe. Then there was Germany's Konrad Adenauer, Italy's Alcide de Gasperi, Belgium's Paul-Henri Spaak, France's Robert Schuman—all men who distrusted even their own nations and who felt that only the largest possible aggregation of countries could lessen the number of dangerous friction points. There was also a unique personality who remains a major figure in European affairs to this day: Joseph M. A. H. Luns was then Foreign Minister of the Netherlands, a job he held for nineteen years before becoming Secretary-General of NATO. At every stage, he has been a leading advocate of the closest possible union, sometimes even standing up to General Charles de Gaulle on the touchiest of issues. And of course there was Jean Monnet, the French economist, perhaps the most persistent driving force and often called the "Father of the Common Market." Heir to a cognac fortune and a lifelong advocate of European co-operation, Monnet formed a loosely knit committee of influential persons from many nations to promote unity. The Monnet Plan, which he pushed with unflagging optimism, proved to be the nucleus of the eventual agreement.

By 1951 these men and their followers had succeeded in forming a "European Coal and Steel Community" to co-ordinate the policies of six countries—France, Germany, Italy, Belgium, the Netherlands, and Luxembourg—on these key industries. It worked well enough to become the springboard for a much bigger leap. While keeping the Coal and Steel Community alive, the leaders of these same six nations met in 1957 and set up the Treaty of Rome, which formed them into the European Economic Community, colloquially called the Common Market. (There is this distinction between the names: the Common Market properly refers only to the tariff and trade arrangements. The term Community implies far broader co-operation on almost all subjects.)

The heart of the Rome Treaty was a promise to reduce duties on all manufactured goods traded among the six countries and to set up a new outer tariff wall between the EEC as a whole and the rest of the world. France's Citroën or Peugeot cars would encounter lower and lower taxes—and soon none at all—when crossing the border to be sold in Italy or the Netherlands. And France's customs duty on, say, an Italian-made refrigerator or a German air conditioner would also drop to zero. Less "protection" for local manufacturers; but more opportunity for any producer with a will to compete and sell throughout Europe. Thus for trading purposes the six would become as one nation, with its temporary capital in Brussels. The "single market" urged by the US a decade earlier was under way. And the agreement contained some futuristic articles expressing the hope that many other monetary, political and social effects would follow.

The key compromise that should be kept in mind to understand much of what came later and what is yet to come was between France and Germany. Bringing these two old foes together was a major reason for the whole plan, after all, and they form the geopolitical heart of the continent. Hidden in the wording of the Rome Treaty is the implication that French farmers would get rich new markets for their products throughout the EEC, in return for France's painful reduction of her high tariff on manufactured goods. And the Germans, who would benefit most from the new customers for their industry, would be sacrificing the interests of their less productive farmers.

The original idea was for a much bigger EEC. But Great Britain seriously misjudged the chances of its success, decided that France and Germany would never co-operate for long, and took no part in the 1957 Rome Treaty. By the time the Macmillan government realized its mistake a few years later, the EEC was thriving, abolishing tariffs and boosting internal trade much faster than expected. The French and some others had begun to feel very dubious about letting in other members who might upset things.

All this while, Washington was making a massive concession, too. In wholeheartedly cheering the success of its brainchild, the US was voluntarily permitting a huge competitor to take shape. Some Europeans found it hard to believe that Americans really wanted a potential rival to grow so great, but their suspicions were unfounded at that time. US officials were focusing on the Soviet menace in those days, and no West European buffer state could be too large or cohesive to suit them.

The speed of the European Community's early development was incredible, and it had profound effects on the policies of many other nations—in Europe, the Americas, and Asia—that are very much a part of the future outlook as seen from this point in the 1970's.

The deceptively simple act of starting to abolish tariffs on most goods traded among the Common Market countries quickly reached into every pocketbook on the entire continent—and far beyond.

The foresighted men who conceived the idea of the European Community anticipated this broad effect, although it is doubtful that even they envisioned its full extent. Jean Monnet and a few others like him were really aiming for political union, but using economics as a foundation. If the fibers of business between the neighbor countries could begin to entwine themselves together firmly enough, they reasoned, there would soon be new ties that could lead to the formation of a new nation.

Some of this transformation did occur at a pace far ahead of the original timetable. If unforeseen new troubles have clouded the outlook for further integration, it is nonetheless important to realize that the business interaction is still at work and affecting the lives of Europeans.

What happened to money and jobs and trade in Europe is an exciting chapter in human history. As soon as companies realized that they would be able to sell all over Europe without paying tariffs at each border, they began to expand their factories, warehouses, truck fleets, and sales offices in neighbor countries. A terrific surge of new investments swept over the six original Common Market members almost at once. Along with expanded facilities, they began to look for the latest technology and machinery, to copy American mass-production methods. When American companies saw this and realized that this big single market in Europe would be somewhat separated from the outside world by a new wall of tariffs around the entire Community, they too rushed in to establish new plants.

Each such factory tended to stimulate business all over Europe, for most modern products are composed of materials and parts from dozens or scores of countries. Picture a General Motors plant in Belgium, for example. It is set up with machinery from the US, Germany, the Low Countries, France, and England. It hires many workers from southern Europe, as well as Belgians. Among its thousands of components, the car that comes through the assembly line contains Dutch steel, Belgian-made glass and spark plugs, German instruments and upholstery material, French tires. The automatic transmissions were first imported from the US, but later factories capable of making these were also erected in Europe. And each plant that produces just one such component must get its materials from hundreds of other suppliers all over the continent and beyond.

One figure alone is enough to show dramatically what the EEC has done to trade among the member countries. It has multiplied nine times over since the Community began. In 1958 less than seven billion dollars' worth of goods were traded annually among the six original member countries. By now, these six alone—not to mention the enlarged Community—trade over sixty billion dollars' worth of products among themselves.

These movements even led to important developments outside the EEC. First, the expanded factories within the Community had become large and efficient enough to be much more competitive in markets all over the world. And second, seven neighboring countries led by Great Britain became so fearful of the Community's growing power that they hastily formed a competitive block of their own, the European Free Trade Association. This group—the United Kingdom, Norway, Sweden, Denmark, Switzerland, Portugal and Austria—had none of the profound political goals of the EEC, but it did cut tariffs, increase trade, and create still more demand for labor. There was a movement of lower-cost workers into not only the Common Market countries, but also into all the industrially developed nations of Europe. These workers came up from the south—from southern Italy, Spain, and Greece, and eventually from Yugoslavia, Lebanon, and Turkey.

So, not only did the cities of Europe begin to bulge with nearby people who had left the farm in order to become factory workers; they also acquired new colonies of Sicilians and Greeks and Turks. Restaurants and movie houses catering to these foreign workers began to spring up in places like Zurich, Frankfort, Amsterdam, and London. At the same time, workers themselves usually sent every spare bit of cash back to their own homes, and this money stimulated business in Spain and Greece and even more distant lands. It also created new buying power and even wider markets for the products of Europe's leading countries.

The net result has been to put a new face on many parts of Europe—more factories, more sterile modern buildings, more rolling vehicles and pollution. Many Europeans don't like this, and sentimental American tourists dislike it even more. But European workers do like their new possessions, and politicans are afraid to suggest that they should be curbed.

Notice that most of this involves *factory-made* products. Agriculture was and is a headache to the planners of the new Europe. They had to make special and enormously cumbersome arrangements for farm goods. In order to keep faith with France, they set up a so-called Common Agricultural Policy that has embroiled them in constant trouble both inside and outside the Community. Member countries make payments into a stabilization fund that keeps farm prices artificially high. But the amounts owed by each country have been distorted every time nations have adjusted the value of their currencies. And the protectionist aspects of the farm policy have occasionally threatened to diminish American agricultural exports to Europe, leading to ugly looks and words between Washington and Brussels. The extreme delicacy of this agricultural tangle among the member countries can be appreciated if we know that eleven per cent of the EEC's population consists of farmers. Considering how much power the farm vote exerts in the US, where it is only four per cent of the electorate, it is not hard to imagine how quickly a European government would fall if it tried to override the wishes of its farming citizens.

Oddly enough, this agricultural dilemma helps to show

how business deals have the potential for creating new political ties; for it has produced one kind of supranationalism that goes beyond what has happened in the industrial field. Some of Europe's less advanced farmers, in Germany, Italy, and the Netherlands, feeling threatened by government policies that aim at phasing them out of existence and promoting big mechanized farms, have occasionally shown great sympathy with each other. They have even demonstrated on behalf of this unity. This is the kind of combination that can start to loosen ties within an old nation and to create a new and broader loyalty. If a Belgian farmer feels closer brotherhood with a German farmer than he does with other Belgians who work in factories, he is beginning to be a new kind of citizen.

But this is cited only as an exceptional phenomenon, and it is by no means typical or community-wide. The French farmer tends to be in the opposite situation. France has developed larger mechanized farms. So French agriculture wants more chance to compete within the EEC—knowing that it can handily defeat the higher-cost products of most other member countries—but wants an outer wall of protection against the even more efficient American farmer. This French position in agriculture is, in fact, one of the main keys to French behavior in the EEC. Charles de Gaulle's frequent threat to walk out of the Community if he didn't get his own way had at least one solid and unemotional reason: France had made a great sacrifice on the industrial side when she signed the Rome Treaty. Her highly protected industries would be hurt by the bigger German factories and the Italian plants that had lower-cost labor. The balancing incentive that French farm goods would gain a much wider market could not be withdrawn. Otherwise, France really would see little reason to go on being a member of the EEC.

17

Brilliant Beginning

Not only in agriculture, but in a good many other lines as well, there have been displays of fraternal feeling that seem to transcend the old frontiers. And some of this certainly makes an occasional appearance among the new corps of EEC civil servants in Brussels, although it is usually cut short in moments of crisis, and it seldom includes the representatives of France. There is also a feeling of unconcern with national boundaries among educators and scientists, but not too much should be made of it, for such has been the way of many thinkers in centuries past.

The area in which the trend to supranational loyalties is potentially of greatest significance is organized labor. There have been a few instances where labor unions in one member country have gone so far as to strike on behalf of demands by fellow workers in another country. But the inflationary threat of this—the boom-and-bust menace that lurks behind it—makes it more an explosive than a cohesive force and will merit a closer look later.

Finally, the economic union has brought the EEC's people closer together by mingling their investments more and more in a common mixing bowl. This trend has been interrupted by the series of monetary crises that required restraints on the movement of capital, but such curbs have not prevented a big increase in company mergers, acquisitions, joint ventures, and international trading in common stocks. Although the occasional failures in business cooperation have often drawn the most public attention, the real news is that so many companies have become really European in scope. And the tendency to borrow outside one's own country if the rate is a bit lower, to sell bond issues throughout the Community, or to move savings to a neighbor country where the interest rate is a little better—these are new habits which, threatened as they are by the current tide of events, will not be entirely forgotten.

For the magnetic effect of Europe's business changes has been profound. There is not one worker in or near the EEC whose wages and life have not been affected by the force. Cities and outlying factories have grown much bigger, pushing new residential areas even farther from town and making most of the population into commuters.

Giannino's restaurant, in Milan, used to give its lunchtime customers peas that had been picked that morning. Now they are still very good, but they are yesterday's vegetables. They come from fifteen kilometers farther away, because the farmland that was once so near is now covered with buildings. There are pros and cons to this: new jobs for the men who truck the food into town, but fewer jobs on the large and mechanized farms. The Milanese have more purchasing power, but it cannot buy them the zesty taste of freshly picked food.

In Paris, the owner of a small jewelry shop near Place Vendôme closes his doors at noon, but stays inside and lunches at an office desk. He used to walk home to an apartment behind the Madeleine, have a large meal and an hour's rest. Now his wife and children are in suburbia—in the modern and expensive Parly II apartment complex—and the drive is too long for a midday break.

Many workers who used to relish their long noonday meal at home and the siesta that followed it now ask for a short lunch hour instead and the right to leave work early for the long trip home. There is hardly an industry, a service trade, a line of business that is quite the same. And because most of these lines deal with America—selling to the US, buying from the US, supplying component parts, or paying patent royalties—no American who owns a share of common stock and few Americans who have jobs are untouched by the waves that emanate from Europe.

And yet, just as the new Europe came to a critical time, America's interest in it had cooled. The nation that had inspired the rebirth of the Old World had suddenly become too absorbed with Southeast Asia to cast more than an occasional irritated glance across the Atlantic.

3

The Wages of Progress

The Vietnam syndrome came at the worst possible moment, when Europe's internal changes made it especially important for the US to be even stronger, gentler, and more adroit in balancing the relationship. Three trends were under way:

· A surfeit of long prosperity brought high economic fever to Europe.

· Russia's new image as a casual, sometimes even genial, neighbor was eroding the common fear that had been the chief foundation of Western cohesion.

· The emergence of a young generation that had no firsthand experience with the old wars was starting to dilute the feeling that NATO and a united Free World defense were vital.

Each of these currents was starting to flow in the mid 1960's. Each of them is now a torrent. And while the first two may well be interrupted by errors in one or more capitals, the third can only become wider and deeper with every passing month.

That prolonged prosperity creates its own kind of trouble is now apparent to all. When first Germany, then Italy and others had "economic miracles" of industrial growth, they seemed delightful—not only to the workers who graduated from bicycles to motor scooters to small cars, but equally so to the wealthy men who made those consumer goods and the stockholders who invested in their companies. Some of the undesirable side effects—clogged cities, congested roads, polluted air—were foreseen and talked about as problems for the future. But a deadlier and less palpable problem was not envisioned. It might be called "polluted government." For the expectation by a whole people that full employment at steadily rising incomes must be a permanent condition of life actually takes some of the main decisions of government out of the hands of the leaders and makes them into automatic, knee-jerk reactions. This is totally different from the ancient problem of politicians who promise one thing and then do another. The fact that high prosperity became a must for all classes meant that really fighting inflation or stabilizing an economy was literally ruled out for elected officials. Interest rates or money supplies might be toyed with, but never the basic factor of how many workers would keep earning larger amounts and bidding up the prices of meat, homes, and fuel.

A strong US might, with great difficulty, have helped to moderate this pernicious course for the whole Western World. Whether or not it had the wisdom, it would have had the weight to force Europeans to adopt more rational policies about their own industrial growth, to make them accept more of Japan's products, for example, at the cost of slowing down their own production. An Atlantic Community that was as firm as it had been in pre-Vietnam days would have barred from the minds of Arabs or Russians any thought of further fueling Western inflation with skyrocketing oil prices. A US President who had the firmness to resist high-employment pressures in his own country might have provided enough support to build similar firmness in Europe's capitals. But President Johnson and then

President Nixon had wobbly home fronts that they had to placate at all costs. And by the time Gerald Ford entered the White House the price spiral in our own country was too far advanced to suppose that Washington could provide guidance to others.

So by this point in the 1970's Europe's inability to fight inflation is accepted as a chronic disease. Even with fuel scarcity as a potential excuse for letting economies slow down, the leaders can manage no more than a token of resistance to the economic flames that are consuming their free capitalist systems. They pretend that it is a great achievement to pull back momentarily from twelve or fifteen per cent inflation to a plateau half that high—which would have been regarded as a disastrous level a year or two earlier. They ignore the fact that even a reduced percentage figure represents *more* inflation piled cumulatively atop that of prior periods. To survive in office they must permit the wage-and-price numbers to keep moving higher. These blight the lives of rich and poor alike—taking away old savings from some and illusory new wages from others. And much of the woe is blamed on America, for the commonest European excuse is that "the US exported its inflation to us."

To that defensible argument has been added the specious claim that Europe's economies were on the point of being controlled when America's Mideast policy spoiled everything. It is not so. For over ten years, no realist could have pretended to see any sign that inflation in Europe was heading for a cure. I was in Europe in the fall of 1973, *before* the fuel crisis that followed the second Arab-Israeli war. It was clear that the inflationary spiral was unchecked even then. Every hotel bill, every meal, every ride was not just a bit higher than it had been the year before, but twenty per cent or thirty per cent higher. Workers I talked with in Italy, Spain, and Switzerland had become as sophisticated and as disenchanted as the bankers and economic ministers. High and low alike, what they said amounted to: "Wages will rise again, and that will send prices higher, and then wages will have to go up some more. Nobody will gain. We can only keep running to delay the time when we all lose."

The doctrine of "peaceful coexistence" enunciated by Nikita Khrushchev was used by his successors to turn a half-century of self-defeating Russian antagonism into a clever foreign policy that has befuddled and mired the West. Probably no leader of our century has made so great an impact on history as Khrushchev. Most statesmen merely leap onto a passing bandwagon and pretend that they are driving it. But Khrushchev reversed the teachings of his own Soviet generation and all the centuries of Czarist isolation to proclaim a whole new approach to trade and profit-making and a new relationship with the outside world. He did not even have any grass-roots sentiments to play on. He merely used his peasant shrewdness to reason that personal incentives boost production, that profits are good economics, and that soft talk is a more effective way to break up allies than saber rattling. It brought him down in the Kremlin, for it turned the military clique against him. But Brezhnev and Kosygin, who overthrew Khrushchev, took the most important pages from his book.

This new USSR, eagerly talking trade with the West, meeting its business obligations punctiliously, welcoming tourists, and repeatedly warning that its main military preoccupation is with China, could not keep serving as a very effective bogeyman. The leaders in Washington and much of Europe—all really wanting to find good reasons for preserving their NATO ties—would feel moments of relief when the Soviets had to show unpopular force as invaders of Czechoslovakia or as supporters of the Arabs against Israel. But the Kremlin always cut those losses skillfully. Russian forces—odious as their presence was—were almost incredibly restrained in Czechoslovakia and withdrawn as rapidly as possible. They managed to avoid putting their own troops into battle in the Mideast or Indo-China. And meanwhile there were the American media telling the world about US bombings of Hanoi and massacres of Vietnamese villagers.

"When will you stop this insanity?" I heard one European diplomat inquire.

"How can we hold NATO together if America seems like the world's worst aggressor?" despaired another.

"Why do you Americans take on the job of containing China—which should be Russia's worry—and leave the Russians free to look like pacifists?" a veteran Belgian foreign ministry official asked me.

All these men and most others like them knew the truth about Russia's continuing military build-up and her globe-girdling naval strategy. But how could they keep their publics aware of an invisible menace? How could they give meaning to an alliance with the nation that was wallowing in self-accusations about extermination bombing and racism?

The passage of time, too, was bound to work against America. Yes, we had saved Europe in war; and yes, we had rebuilt her after the war. But that sunshine of yesteryear was unknown to millions of young voters. Even when the Treaty of Rome was signed, in 1957, the Europeans just turning twenty-one were people who had been only nine years old when World War II ended. By the mid 1960's these members of the body politic were going into their thirties, and behind them at the polling places were millions who were not even born when the war ended. And so even the need for a North Atlantic Treaty Organization—the alliance of America, Canada, and all Western Europe except Sweden and Switzerland—was cast into doubt. It had held firm against years of attempted Russian encroachment, but its relevance to the 1970's was questioned by the very young. "We are dealing not only with people who don't remember the World Wars," NATO Secretary-General Joseph Luns told me, "but also with younger voters who don't even remember the Cold War. When we talk about an outside threat, they are more likely to think of America than Russia. The Americans they can see. The Russians are less visible and much quieter."

Such was the stage setting when the US voluntarily abandoned its role. The bulk of European workers were growing accustomed to fattening wages, a growing pile of material possessions, and steady inflation as a way of life. Their offspring were growing up with a shoulder-shrugging attitude toward many traditional values and a distaste for America. The Soviets were staying in the wings and gradually pulling offstage that image of a great monster which had given the drama its chief significance.

That America would leave the other players on their own was foreshadowed by the 1965 decision to stay in Vietnam at any price. But the practical sign of this was not given until a shocking moment in 1967. The "Kennedy Round" of tariff-cutting negotiations had gone on for nearly five years. It was supposed to do for the entire modern world what the Common Market arrangements had done for much of Europe—extend the trade-boosting effect of lower tariffs to all industrial nations and head off any tendency for the EEC or any other group to become an isolated oasis of freer trade. The US had initiated the idea and gamely went on with the negotiations to the end. The massive multination agreement was signed with great ceremony, and Washington even promised to ask Congress for further duty-lowering measures. But those measures were never seriously pushed, because even before the Kennedy Round ended the US economy was in deep trouble. A prominent African diplomat who was present on the festive day recently confessed to me that he turned to a colleague and said, "This is all a sham. America cannot possibly keep these trade promises." The signing had been a hollow anachronism.

Less than three months after the great ceremony, the Johnson Administration was demanding that Europe give the US an across-the-board cut in tariffs on American products to help us sell more there! It was as if a man went through with signing a contract to buy a home, even after knowing that his income was being cut, and then almost immediately began to insist on a lowering of the price and the mortgage payments.

European leaders were aghast and in great disarray. The almost unheard-of reversal and admission of weakness, coming from a nation they had grown to think of as all-powerful, made them react negatively. Yet when they looked at the hard business facts they saw themselves trapped. America's balance of payments really was getting into dangerous red ink. The US really should sell more and spend less abroad—even if only to protect the value of the dollars that Europe itself was holding. But Europe could not increase its purchases or cut its sales or suck in fewer tourists from America without hurting its own prosperity. That might even raise the awful specter of heavy *unemployment* in Europe. Better to soft-pedal the complaints about America's adverse balance of payments. Let the dollars keep flowing to Europe and worry later about their diminishing value.

So it started—the mistrust, the furtiveness, the secret pretense that all was essentially sound—when in fact the heads of government were acting like bank employees who keep their jobs by doctoring the books and hoping that some miracle will save them before their shortages are discovered. Deeper and deeper into debt such people always go. And as they do, their hands are more tightly tied. By the late 1960's Europe even had to swallow the Nixon Administration's proclamation of a doctrine called "benign neglect." "The dollars in Europe are Europe's problem, not ours," said Washington. "There's no reason for us to change our domestic policies to suit Europe." Shocked and angered by the new theory that a debtor's promissory notes are something for only the creditor to worry about, the leaders of Europe still could find no way to fight back. Not without risking a dent in their employment figures.

And so the relationship between Europe and America stood when, in 1973, the EEC made a great gesture of its own. At age fifteen, the European Community made the long-awaited move of admitting Britain to full membership. The Republic of Ireland and Denmark joined at the same time, so that six members suddenly became nine. In adding three new members, the Community dared to hope that a new surge of progress was now in the making. To grow by fifty per cent, to link Britain with the continent, to create a market of over 250 million people—these were accomplishments as dramatic as the EEC's early successes. But were they as solidly cemented? Did they point as convincingly toward even more development along the same lines? No. They had the look of reflex actions—less vigorous, less meaningful than those of the past.

This collection of people is, none the less, the largest trading bloc in the world. In health or in sickness, it is a massive force in determining how well the rest of us live. It accounts for over twenty-five per cent of all the international trade in the world. It also buys over one-fourth of all US exports and provides about twenty-three per cent of all US imports. Seen as a group and from a distance, it is an immense market of some 255 million consumers, all with rising desires and rising incomes to buy more goods. Whatever this may mean for the future in terms of intensifying pollution and overcrowded roads, the statistics of growth are a delight to businessmen and politicians, who can seldom afford the luxury of thinking ahead for more than a few years at a time.

Even with its original six members, the Common Market had been a great trade magnet, a market big enough to attract investments and win concessions from all the other major nations. But then Europe was sharply divided; the seven countries of the European Free Trade Association were ranged against the EEC. Companies setting up industrial plants in Europe were not quite sure whether to put them into one or the other of these groups, and very often they procrastinated and put off the investment altogether. Other nations of the Western Hemisphere or Asia had to be sure to divide their favors and their plans for the future. Now, essentially, the European Economic Community *is* Europe. That it is directionless and losing much of its early promise must not disguise its vast residual importance. Even a crippled giant can have enormous needs and great weight. The other countries around its periphery have had to make special agreements in order that their trade can continue at all. Nations even as far away as the Middle East and Africa have become associate members so that upward of thirty countries have special links of one kind or another to the EEC. It is not an empire, but no other nation of our time has so widely spread a network. This fact alone, and the commercial significance that flows from it, heightens the dismay we must feel at recalling America's veer away from Europe and toward greater emphasis on other areas.

4

The "Government" of Europe

In Brussels, a ten-minute cab ride away from the city's business center, are two modern high-rise office buildings surrounded by a large paved plaza. This is the physical capitol of the European Economic Community, rather bare, all glass and cement, typifying the stark changes which some say the EEC is working in Brussels itself and all over Europe.

The people who work in these offices have made some very respectable moves in the direction of managing Europe internally. They go beyond any other international effort of our time—far beyond the force and solidity of the United Nations, for example, or of attempts to bring Arab or Latin-American nations closer together.

At least three major steps toward central government have already exceeded expectations: a European budget that puts a growing sum of money at the disposal of the officials in Brussels; a program for community-wide aid to the unemployed; and a common fund for developing the backward areas of each country. These represent a small, but germinal, pooling of interests and sacrifice of national prerogatives.

Having the right to raise money and spend it independently could be a major indicant that a real government is emerging. As of now the EEC's power along this line is barely beginning. Although its budget—contributed by member states in proportion to their GNP—amounts to about four and one-half billion dollars annually, the greatest part of that sum consists of a fund for supporting farm prices. Some four hundred million dollars are allowed for the work of the Commission, the Council of Ministers, Parliament, a Court of Justice, and an atomic-research program. Most of the money that the EEC controls, therefore, is to pay for its own administrative costs and involves little discretionary outlay. But the Commission has two other spending powers that are embryonically significant: to disburse substantial amounts for food aid to poorer countries, and to control a quarter-billion-dollar European Social Fund aimed at facilitating the mobility of workers and easing problems that arise from social changes.

This Social Fund deserves special attention, because any step toward pooling and redistributing money to large numbers of people can be the start of a chain reaction.

At a Paris summit meeting in 1972 it was declared that the nine EEC governments "attach as much importance to vigorous action in the social field as to the achievement of economic and monetary union." No one took much notice of this, but the implications are substantial.

The first steps taken were an increased program of vocational training and more social services for migrant workers. The Social Fund helps the handicapped to acquire useful abilities and unemployed persons to learn new skills. Farm workers who wish to leave the agricultural field and textile workers who lose their jobs are trained for new occupations.

Perhaps the most dramatic form of assistance so far has been to unemployed coal miners, who are aided by a special fund of the European Coal and Steel Community. Such men are paid seventy-five to eighty per cent of their former salaries for a period of up to thirty months while waiting for new jobs or working at lower-paying ones. The ECSC also helps to pay for retraining and to attract new industries that can give jobs to the former miners. As a consequence, thousands of men who were working underground just a short time ago—or not working at all—have changed to blue-collar operations in much more normal environments.

Eighty men who had worked in the dwindling mines of Limbourg, Holland, for example, were given a chance to learn a very complex technical skill—producing engraved plates for printing color photos. People in the graphic industry scoffed at the idea that miners, whom they considered slow-witted and loath to change, could make the switch. But although the older men did have great difficulty, seventy-nine of the eighty passed the government proficiency test. One of them, Fred Jensen, has gone on to become head of the photo department of an important plant. "You get only one chance like this," says Jensen. "It had to be done, and we did it."

One other radical departure is a regional development program that also involves the controversial concept of making people of one area contribute tax money for help to those of a poorer region. It is noteworthy that anything of this sort—so painful even within a single nation like the US—has been begun in the nine-nation EEC. There is no use pretending that it has gone easily. A disagreement about contributions—that should have been decided by the last day of 1973—was so knotty that the ministers "stopped the clock" and ruled that the year had not officially ended. Far into January 1974 the impasse lasted, and insiders were referring to the date as December 45th, December 50th, and so on. But the fact that agreement on such a set of conflicting interests is even attempted is historic.

It had originally been proposed that each member state should receive from the fund the same amount of money that it contributed. But that was seen to be an exercise in futility, and a start on the basis of need was made with an initial sum of about five hundred million dollars. It was clear to the Germans, for example, that their contribution would go much more to benefit Britain, Italy, and Ireland than to help any part of Germany. The rational argument given for this is that by balancing up economic growth and eliminating some of the worst depressed areas urban congestion would be reduced and the whole Community would benefit.

Aid from the fund goes to rural areas that are too dependent on low-productivity farming and to areas that are handicapped by old and declining industries. The money is used mainly for industrial projects and for building roads or other fundamental public works that are necessary before new factories can be attracted.

In evaluating the importance of these spending powers, bear in mind that none of them is in the hands of persons *elected* to their jobs. They are given to appointed officials—bodies of men designated by their home governments who can be withdrawn at will. So Paris, Rome, Bonn, et cetera keep a very tight rein on the money they allocate. This means an equally fast hold on the decisions made in Brussels. The line between the right to make policies and the duty to implement the policies of others is still sharply drawn in Europe. It is what makes Brussels a center, and not truly a capital, up to this moment.

The EEC government revolves around a thirteen-member Commission, with two appointees each from West Germany,

France, Italy, and Britain, and one from each of the five smaller nations. This Commission—which meets each Wednesday—is headed by a President. The right to fill this top office is rotated among the member countries.

At the moment of expanding to nine countries, for example, the presidency went to France. François-Xavier Ortoli, a tough Gaullist politician who had been Minister of Industrial and Scientific Development in the Paris government, moved into the top Brussels post. His own new cabinet included British diplomat Sir Christopher Soames, heading EEC foreign policy, and such other colleagues as German Ralf Dahrendorf, a brilliant young sociology professor, Italian Altiero Spinelli, a socialist lawyer who once spent ten years in jail for antifascist activities, Luxembourg's Albert Borschette, a Ph.D. and award-winning novelist, and Ireland's Patrick Hillery, a medical doctor who moved belatedly into politics and rose rapidly to become his country's foreign minister. A brilliant group, in short, more intellectual and broad-gauged than the average national cabinet, because these are mostly men whose interests extend beyond parochial politics. They also extend beyond the problems of the moment—sufficient as those are for the tastes of most politicians. However frustrated by their home governments, they do keep trying to reach a bit farther than the expedient solutions of the current fiscal year.

Under the President and his cabinet is a budding bureaucracy of six thousand civil servants, who are often referred to as "Eurocrats"—many of them able to handle all three of the Community's official languages, French, German, and English. There is a formula for splitting up these jobs among the nations: Denmark and Ireland each name five per cent of the personnel; each of the other nations appoints eighteen per cent of the workers (with Belgium, the Netherlands, and Luxembourg being counted as one member for this purpose). But then the countries have to fight hard for the prize portfolios on the Commission. There is active logrolling and compromising to decide on which "cabinet posts" each Commissioner will hold—such as external affairs, monetary affairs, or agriculture. Equally spirited is the struggle for lesser staff assignments that have considerable influence on European affairs. A steady process of internal politicking decides what nationalities will control key desks—as deputies to commissioners, heads of departments, and so on.

This is a turn away from the original idea that the Eurocrats would all but forget their national origins and become true civil servants of a new Europe. It was unrealistic, despite the enthusiasm that many individuals really did bring to Brussels, because their home governments still controlled their jobs. A Eurocrat who so far forgot himself as to differ with the official view of his own capital on a certain issue was not apt to hold his Brussels job for long. So a policy of acknowledging the competition among nationalities now prevails, and it is rationalized as being a more realistic path to eventual unification.

It is important to keep a clear distinction between the *Commission* and the EEC's other main ruling body. All major decisions are actually made by the *Council of Ministers*—meaning representatives of the member governments. While the Commission members are *appointed* by their home governments, the Council members are actually the foreign ministers of those separate governments. And the fact that key moves are reserved for them emphasizes that no nation has yet relinquished its sovereign rights—not even to a body that it helps to appoint. But in practice any action must first be proposed by the Commission. So the composition and the enthusiasm of that group can make a great difference. A Commission that persists in proposing radical measures might greatly embarrass any member government that repeatedly had to veto the ideas. In the EEC's first years, in fact, when Germany's Walter Hallstein was its President, the Commission was so active and full of initiative that it seemed to presage another case of a strong executive shaping the office to new dimensions, as happened early in US history. But succeeding Presidents were either men of lesser stature or were frustrated by member nations that wanted no such power in Brussels.

The paramount importance of each country's own government is demonstrated by the numerous instances when an official has left a major post in the EEC to go back to his home parliament. Franco Maria Malfatti, for example, resigned as President of the EEC when general elections were called in Italy; going back to maintain his seat in the Italian parliament was much more vital to his future. Not long after that, Sicco Mansholt similarly quit the EEC's top post in order to return to Dutch politics. The fact that a political base in a single nation far outweighs the career importance of even the top post in Brussels forces us to realize that the point where real sovereign power begins to shift to a supranational authority has not yet been approached.

Also part of the EEC's government is the European Parliament. It has the least present power, but the most intriguing future. This body's history is long as EEC affairs go, because it was named in the 1951 treaty that formed the European Coal and Steel Community—forerunner of the EEC by six years. That agreement stipulated that the High Authority of the ECSC was to be accountable to a "Common Assembly." It began with seventy-eight members and first met in September 1952. Later, when the Rome Treaty added the European Economic Community and an atomic authority called Euratom, it made all three communities subject to a larger body, which is now known as the "European Parliament." It has 142 members, ranging from thirty-six each for the main nations down to six representatives for Luxembourg. These members group themselves into four broad parties: Christian Democrats, Socialists, Liberals (which, in Europe, means economic conservatives), and French Gaullists, plus a few Italian Communists. Surprisingly, the representatives usually vote a party line rather than a national one.

The European Parliament is not yet a proper legislative body for two reasons: it is only *selected* from among the legislators of each country—not elected by the people. And it has few real powers. When it meets for several week-long sessions each year in Strasbourg, France, it is largely a debating group, with no legislation to pass on and hardly any financial powers. A small amount of budgetary authority was given in the early 1970's—for the financing of the Community's own institutions—which involves about five per cent of the EEC's total appropriations.

The Parliament's most important power under the Rome Treaty is the right to censure the Commission by a two-thirds vote. Because of the parliamentary principle that a government resigns when it loses a confidence vote, this theoretically gives Europe's Parliament the right to fire the Commission. But up to now this power has never been used, and it is seriously diluted by the fact that Parliament cannot touch the Council of Ministers—the body that actually makes all the key decisions.

There is much talk of changing this. In mid 1972 a committee headed by French constitutional expert Georges Vedel proposed direct universal European suffrage, meaning that all the EEC's voters would go to the polls at one time to elect their representatives to the European Parliament—persons chosen just for that purpose, and not doing dual duty at the national level. Even before that, said the Vedel Report, the Parliament should get some real powers. It should have the right to ratify or disapprove decisions of the Council of Ministers in revising Community treaties, admitting new members, and concluding international agreements. It should also have the power to delay the Council's actions and to force it to deliberate further. Later on, it is proposed that Parliament have full decision-making power over the EEC's farm, transport, and commercial policies, rules of business competition, harmonization of laws and tax systems, and the mushrooming European Social Fund.

If these changes all came about, it would mean a truly major step toward nationhood. We can imagine the separate national governments rather rapidly becoming less important, while the members of a European Parliament—responsible to no one but the voters back home—would begin to press popular social legislation and enlarge its authority by pleasing the masses. It is precisely this diminution of national government roles that will constantly act as a drag on real European unity. Politicians who have succeeded in reaching high places in their own nations are no more anxious than other men to lose their jobs or cut their own authority.

Like so many institutions, the Common Market has been developing in ways that neither its creators nor its present officials could foresee. It seems almost to have a will of its own, independent of the bureaucracy that tries to rule it from Brussels. This bureaucracy, though not quite a government, is much like most governments. It has established embassies (although it calls them "delegations") in most of the world's major capitals; and it receives ambassadors from many countries. It has even had brushes with scandal. A few million dollars from the EEC budget have been misplaced and never accounted for. Civil servants in different divisions accuse each other of ineptness. The enthusiasm that most of them felt for the great new Europe which they were determined to build has been frayed by the near impossibility of getting anything decided among nine governments.

"You have no idea how frustrating it is to try to get nine capital cities to agree on even the smallest point," one high official of the EEC told me. "In order to decide what we are going to say to a non-member capital like Stockholm or Madrid on some minor issue, we sometimes have to circulate a draft twelve or fourteen times. Then this carefully worded document is sent to that other country, and if it suggests the smallest change, we have to start the whole process of agreeing among ourselves again."

And yet, somehow, these neighboring Europeans with such different attitudes and ways have managed to adapt to this unlikely co-operation. A German member of the Brussels hierarchy told me: "The Treaty of Rome says the same thing to all members, but it works very differently in each nation. Take the movement of goods between countries. We all know that many types of products are supposed to move right through the borders without tariff and without interruption. Between Germany and France or Germany and the Netherlands, that's exactly what they do. But what do you think happens when that same type of product comes to the Italian frontier? Very often it goes nowhere. The customs officers move the merchandise to one side and let it stand there until some interested party comes along and puts a little money into an upturned palm. Then it goes on its way quickly. Well, that's Italy, and we've all become used to it and learned to our surprise that their way works about as well as our way. So we have developed a tolerance and even a certain fondness for each other."

Looked at in human terms, then, the European Community is a rather awkward bureaucracy trying to manage a collection of peoples with very different characteristics. By most logical standards, it should have failed before now. But instead it has worked tolerably well in providing a central authority for most practical internal problems. This is largely because the peoples involved all have histories of adapting themselves to challenges and operating structured societies.

Now, however, this remarkable organization faces sophisticated challenges—in the fields of money, fuel, and foreign policy—that will embroil the EEC constantly with America, Russia, the Arab world, and Japan. They will be a much more arduous test of Europe's will to unite and the Atlantic Community's ability to survive.

5

The Struggle to Lead

Apart from business questions, the deeper issue for the US and the world is: where will the spirit of the EEC lead next?

Especially now that it is shaking off American influence, will the Community become inward-looking and "nationalistic," or open and friendly to the outside world?

The optimists, once again, are strongly led by Jean Monnet's opinion: "What happened when the Common Market expanded from six members to nine was much more than a mere enlargement," he told me. "It is England's joining that means so much. The country that has influenced world policies for so many centuries is not now planning to hide herself in Europe just for business purposes. England and the other countries of the new Europe will now reach out to influence the world."

No one ever publicly comes out with the opposite view, but the argument for narrowness does exist. Many European leaders stress the need for first protecting Europe's interests before troubling about relations with outsiders. It is the continuing quiet struggle over two issues in Brussels which Americans and others must watch as a prime indication of the Western World's future:

First, will Europe keep moving toward unification as a

new nation, or—since a hoop that stops rolling cannot stand —will it collapse into so many separate states?

Second, if Europe does stay together, will it be world-oriented or isolationist?

The answer to these questions depends on *what nation leads the EEC.* The standard official reply in Brussels is, "No nation, we hope. If any one of us starts to dominate, the organization will fall apart and there will be no Europe."

The history of human institutions shows that this cannot be the answer. If any one power begins to dominate too quickly, too obviously, or too intensely, then it is true that the others will rebel and either form opposing factions or drift apart entirely. But any new nation or new organization that survives and eventually goes on to success gradually forms the habit of being guided by one part of its membership that has more wealth, power, or managerial skill.

The Common Market originally had two members who expected to become its leaders. The Germans secretly believed that their hard work and efficiency would make them masters of the EEC. The French were equally sure that their diplomatic skill would make them the guiding force. And, so far, the French have come closest to being right. Germany's overwhelming industrial and economic successes have led the other nations to regard her as a problem. Throughout the 1960's and early 1970's they made repeated demands on Bonn, and German governments made many concessions, while winning very little in return. But the French, more by firmness and diplomatic dexterity than by material performance, have tended to put their own stamp on Europe.

The French operate like the law professor who advised his students: "If your case is weak on facts, stress the law.

If you are weak on legal points, stress the facts. If you are weak on both, pound the table." When France wanted to dilute EEC antimonopoly rules, she picked on the minutiae of Rome Treaty wording. When she wanted to weaken Washington's hold on Europe, she stressed a vague Gaullist vision of "Europe from the Atlantic to the Urals." And when Paris wanted to assert independence without really giving up American protection, she ordered NATO to move elsewhere. Not a constructive policy, perhaps, but by usually taking the initiative Paris has at least given the impression of having a policy when the others had none. And so the image of the Common Market, the development into a collection of countries that keep their individuality, and the attitude toward the outside world—all these have been chiefly of French origin.

Now a third great power aspires to leadership. Britain entered Europe pretending to be humble and unambitious; but few doubt Jean Monnet's conviction that London has no thought of giving up its old influence over world affairs. And when it comes to diplomatic ability, the British are a match for the French. The French look far ahead to form their own advance image of how the world should go, and then use precise logical arguments to rule out other courses. They also are masters at pretending that they would be quite willing to pull out and go it alone if they failed to get their own way. British diplomacy depends largely, as it always has, on forcing others to underestimate England's position, power, and resolve. By understating, by showing an open mind to everyone's views, and occasionally poking fun at their own, they invariably succeed in throwing even the wariest opponent off guard.

This, after all, is how the British got into the EEC. They waited patiently until France finally had a reason for wanting Britain in—that is, the French realization that German economic power might overwhelm the rest of the continent after all. Then, always adept in the uses of adversity, England was seen to be deeply divided about whether it wanted to join at all. Its negotiating team in Brussels, carefully avoiding any displays of brilliance or aggressiveness, pointed to its troubles back home and waited for the continental countries to offer better and better terms. Unusually good promises were exacted for special treatment of Commonwealth countries. New Zealand's ability to sell her agricultural products in Europe, for example, was protected by EEC concessions that frankly surprised most observers.

The touchy issue of renegotiating Britain's membership terms has been handled with equal dexterity. It was a political necessity for Harold Wilson to make a pretense at this in order to quell the anti-EEC forces in his own party, but it was done most discreetly. The British representatives in Brussels made it clear in private talks that they were anxious not to upset their EEC membership and would only require enough concessions to placate their own home front.

After Britain's entry an interesting two-to-one split developed among the three candidates for leadership. For a time the Britons and Germans were usually together against the French on fundamental issues. This was true on monetary questions, the farm problem, the search for a joint policy on petroleum, and a number of issues involving the Community's external affairs.

Later, when Helmut Schmidt became German Chancellor and Valéry Giscard d'Estaing French President, the two men used their personal friendship to attempt a different combination—reviving the idea of Franco-German co-operation as the core of the EEC. Either of these two-power partnerships would be powerful. But the EEC will not be headed by a team of two. Sooner or later, one will be found to be the pacesetter, or else the organization will fail.

So much for the maneuvering abilities of the contenders for power. What about the practical realities?

France is in the weakest position of the three would-be leaders. Her gross national product is much less than Germany's, though substantially larger than England's. Her performance in controlling wages and prices has been markedly poorer than Germany's, and the overseas territories that France can boast are mainly African nations that are incapable of contributing greatly to France's strength.

Britain, on the other hand, does still have important overseas connections, even if she can no longer claim an empire. As a symbol of how important these can be, bear in mind the fact that Britain's assets and income from investments in India are considerably greater now than they were in imperial times. And this is so in many of the Commonwealth areas that no longer seem closely tied to Britain. Partly as a result of this, Britain's finances include a massive amount of "invisible" earnings, reflecting London's position as the leading center of international insurance, shipping, merchant banking, and other services that help the world to function. When the newspapers gloomily record another British trade deficit, they overlook the fact that trade deficits were the rule even in Britain's wealthiest days. For most of the last two centuries Britain bought much more from abroad than she sold. Invisible earnings made up the difference, and they are still an important element in the equation. Moreover, Britain's inflation and labor troubles have been somewhat exaggerated, though they certainly are serious. Average monthly earnings in Britain approximately doubled between the early 1960's and the early

1970's. But so did those of France; and Germany's were only a little better. "We have always been such an orderly country," a leading British publisher told me, "that when a few hundred men walk down the street with signs, the press calls it a riot." The lag in industrial production and the increase in consumer prices that Britain permitted herself in those critical 1960's is certainly setting the country back considerably. 1975 and perhaps 1976 will be hard times for the British nation. But the great oil and gas discoveries in the North Sea should more than offset that disadvantage by the last years of this decade.

When it comes to industrial power, Germany, even divided as she is from her eastern portion, has been much stronger than any of the others. Perhaps it is not so much efficiency as a genuine liking for hard work that makes Germany more productive. Whatever the cause, German metal products and machinery are impressive. Even a nontechnical observer can admire the solidity and durability of most German goods. And Germany has a special relationship with East Europe that is a major asset. Her trade ties with Russia and the Eastern European satellites are far closer than those of any other Western country, and many a company that wants to trade with the communist world does it through a West German subsidiary. These links with well-located nations that are emerging into modern status may well be much more important assets than ties that Britain and France have with their former colonies. The fact is that if Germany were managed by French officials or represented by British diplomats, there would be little doubt about the future leadership of the European Community. But as it is, the awkwardness of German officialdom undermines the nation's strengths. Keenly aware of their old reputation for arrogance, they have often leaned over backward to let others dominate. They allowed De

Gaulle to stage-manage the public displays of a French-German alliance, let France have her own way repeatedly on the franc-mark exchange rate, made overgenerous concessions to Washington on paying US troop costs in Germany, and have been more willing than any other major country to help neighbors with development costs or to let competitive products come in. This will not last. It is changing now. But the continuing tendency of German leaders either to underplay or overplay their hand must be taken for granted. And Germany will be either the docile rich man of Europe or the intolerable troublemaker.

If forced to make the difficult choice, I would forecast that Britain will lead, even though much of this may be from behind the scenes. I expect, for one thing, that Britain will finally have its own "economic miracle" before 1980—twenty years or so after the Germans and Italians had theirs. If, under the sting of new competition with Europe, British industry finally achieves the modernization that the government has been urging, London's men in Brussels will hold new high cards. But even in the absence of miracles, it must be borne in mind that the British nation as a whole is far from being as behind the times as the Victorian charm of London makes many people believe. A very astute diplomat confided to me after four years as Belgium's Economic Minister in London, "The British are very different from most of us on the continent, but my estimate of their future went up every year that I was there. They have a character and a discipline that is worth much more than all the 'productivity' that economists like to measure. I think they still have the same kind of strength that has always made them hang on and win the final battle. And if you want something more tangible than that, just bear in mind that they are the most technologically advanced nation in Europe. Does that surprise you? Yes, it is true. When it comes to nuclear technology, computer sciences, or aircraft production, they are second only to the Americans."

If Britain should indeed become the leading force in Europe, then we might expect at least some of its neighbors to be outward-looking, thinking more about relations with the world than separating themselves from the world. That is the history of British policy and the nature of the men Britain has sent to Brussels. It is worth remembering that one of its first goals on achieving membership was to gain the foreign-affairs portfolio for an appointee of its choosing. And despite some conscious strategic attempts to obscure the fact, it should also be noted that Britain's centuries-old "special relationship" with America is alive and likely to remain so.

6

Forces Pulling Europe Together

The European Community has more than once been in danger of falling apart. One of its most perilous periods is just ahead. But an assessment of the future must take into account the inner magnetism that has held the pieces in place up to now.

It is the twentieth century, more than anything else, that has been pulling the separate countries of Europe toward each other. It is not only a certain set of leaders or a particular treaty that draws them closer. The same articles, had they been agreed to in Rome some decades earlier, would have been fruitless. The same men would have been powerless to enforce them. The time was made right by the way we live in this portion of history.

"The truth is that Europe makes much more progress toward unity outside the framework of the Rome Treaty than by means of political agreements in Brussels," EEC Commissioner Ralf Dahrendorf told me. "Even when we are having a big crisis in the Commission and members are officially quarreling, dozens of little practical compromises are being made by people at lower levels who find that life simply must go on—and the life of our time cannot be broken up into tiny units."

Here are some of the pressures that transcend boundaries:

· The sprawl of multinational companies with little or no allegiance to any one nation.

· The tangle of new legal relationships and the problems that this creates.

· The sweeping movements of workers from one country to another, and the tendency this produces to equalize conditions among the nations.

· The mountain of documents and computerized information that is growing almost out of control.

· The spreading network of international education.

· Much-publicized demands for higher living standards.

· The ability of more Europeans to travel all over the continent.

· A critical need for safety on the roads.

The growth of multinational companies is both a result of the EEC and a cause of even more unification. It is clear enough that the pulling together of many nations has spurred the growth of bigger companies to take advantage of larger markets. But then the many branches that such firms set up in various nations began to move managers from one country to another. A young German junior executive who hears of a higher opening in the Brussels office asks for a chance at that job. Perhaps an Englishman who has proved himself at home becomes Deputy Managing Director of that same Brussels operation. He likes the young German and later recommends him for a middle management position in Manchester. The company head happens to be Dutch and the firm is technically based in the Netherlands. But as a substantial part of its managers and a major part of its sales are from other countries, its nationality becomes very blurred. This has reached the extreme point where traditionalists angrily charge that multinational companies have no patriotism—and some of the companies proudly answer that it's absolutely true. As the president of Ford International once said, "We have dozens of flags. If you don't like this particular one, we'll deal with you under one of the others."

Needless to say, nations whose business leaders have such affiliations and attitudes do tend to be drawn together. The force is not an all-conquering one. And some nationalities, notably the French, show more immunity to it than others. But the lobbying that used to be almost all in favor of protectionism and a strict separation of national interests is now often opposed by new lobbies pressing for more porous frontiers—freer flow of goods, more interchangeability of labor forces, fewer restrictions on anything "foreign," so that the word itself comes to have less meaning.

As businesses become pan-European, so does business law. One of the early attempts to mesh the business rules in the EEC countries was in the field of antitrust. It had been agreed very early in the Common Market's life that companies in each member country would turn over information about their operations to an antitrust policing unit in Brussels, so that rules against monopolistic practices could apply equally to all. The French fairly soon stunned their partners by saying that they didn't interpret the agreement as the others did; they refused to turn over details about their companies, insisting that other nations might gain a competitive advantage. This was, in fact, the first indication that France would continue to think of itself as a separate nation and not as a unit to be blended into a new country. Nevertheless, the EEC persisted in pressing its antitrust policy and gradually toughening it. This, too, markedly affects American companies. Some of them feel caught between the differing competitive rules of Europe and the US. They may go into joint ventures with European partners and find that an operation which is perfectly legal in Europe violates US antimonopoly laws. But sometimes it is the other way around and the subsidiary of an American firm gets into trouble at the European end. Continental Can, Burroughs, and Parke-Davis are among the US corporations that have been involved in EEC antitrust actions. Pittsburgh Plate Glass and Corning Glass, to take another example, found that their joint subsidiary, Pittsburgh Corning Europe, had been fined $108,000 for selling glass insulating material in Germany at a higher price than in Belgium and Holland. The point is that a legal authority in Brussels can take action and collect a fine as though the countries of Europe were so many states in a single sovereign union.

A much broader legal effect than mere antimonopoly rules is on the way. As the lives of Europe's peoples become so much more interwoven with each other, many of the laws have to change to fit the situation. As of early 1973, in fact, a historic change went into effect, entirely unnoticed: *a person's nationality is no longer a factor in deciding civil or commercial judgments within the Community.* When there are legal actions between persons of different countries there are often questions about which judge or which court is competent to hear the case. But now in the EEC a person comes under the jurisdiction of the country where he lives, regardless of his nationality. It is like saying that for this particular purpose his nationality is simply European.

Of all the unifying factors, multinational labor is probably the weightiest in *potential* importance. It cannot yet be said to have pulled countries together nearly as much as travel and business; but if the unions and the other laboring elements should continue their tendency to co-operate and work toward a continent-wide approach, the effects would alter the very roots of European life.

Start with the fact that Europe, if it can stagger through the mid 1970's recessions, will continue to be hard-pressed to fill its jobs. Owing to a relatively low birth rate in recent decades, the under-twenty-five population will decline. Even after filling many new jobs from Spain, Portugal, Yugoslavia, and even Turkey—which will soon be supplying over a million members of the European work fôrce—the continent will still be undermanned, if present economic trends persist. This means that labor, if it pulls together, could be in a position to dictate terms in Europe. Already a European Confederation of Syndicates has been formed, bringing together over thirty million workers from all nine of the EEC nations, plus five other countries.

The Commission of the European Community—its executive body—feels impelled to move at the vanguard of such a popular impulse, regardless of its dangerous implications. It has issued guidelines for co-ordinating many social policies by the end of 1976—for promoting "full and better employment" by contributing to the creation of new jobs in backward regions, helping member nations to establish retraining programs with guarantees against income loss, setting up a European center for vocational training, assuring housing, education, and other protection to migrant workers, and tackling women's employment problems. It plans to go further and examine minimum wages in the whole Community, possible abolition of assembly-line work, and Community support for unemployment benefits.

Enticing goals, although each embodies the specter of economic and social and environmental suffocation that an excess of such "progress" has always caused before. But good or bad, the thrust of this is in the direction of European integration—either under prosperous capitalism or after an antidemocratic tidal wave that levels Europe's boundaries along with its way of life. Organized labor is potentially the most powerful frontier-bursting force in Europe.

The list of inward-pulling factors could go on at great length. Although each one is small in relation to the size of Europe's current ills, they deserve to be recognized. There are special university programs that enable students to be exchanged among many of the EEC countries. A Council for European Studies even gives fellowships to American graduate students who plan Ph.D. work on a European subject. There is heavy research into the problem of handling the mass of scientific and technological information, which is proliferating three times as fast as anyone expected, owing to the greater international co-operation among researchers. There are attempts to teach more European languages in each country, and even some early efforts to set up publications for the whole continent.

More general, but also profound, is the common conviction that higher living standards must be spread to all men. What Adlai Stevenson called "the revolution of rising expectations" has been occurring not only in backward countries, but much closer to home than we usually think. It touches not only the African or the Latin-American peon who wants a life like the one he hears about on his transistor radio; it happens also in the minds of Europeans who had thought themselves well off until they heard of benefits available to the people of a neighbor country—or of the USA.

Take consumer protection, for example. The very term was unknown in most of Europe until a few years ago. "Let the buyer beware" was considered a very reasonable rule of life. Then the Swedish institution of the Ombudsman and the American-originated notion that governments should do much more to protect consumers from business spread to England and the continent. It was accompanied by a feeling that citizens should band together if the government failed to do its part. And by 1972 officials of the whole Western World were getting together at international conferences to agree on "the need to protect the consumer and to reinforce his power to fight back against deceptive and unfair practices, hazards to safety and health." No nation, however probusiness its government, would dare to stay away from such a conference or to render a dissenting opinion. Its own people would hear of it and be sure that its officials care less for them than for big business.

And perhaps the most direct and tangible factor is travel and all that flows from it. Apart from any idealistic notion that people who get to know each other will be friendlier, very practical changes must be made when so many Europeans are crisscrossing on roads and in the air. Even if fuel problems curtail these numbers somewhat, they remain huge, as does their impact.

The Transport Ministers of the European nations, for example, have been working together increasingly on auto and road safety. They try to standardize rules on road traffic, signs and signals, and speed limits. They develop parallel safety-education programs and first-aid procedures. They even fix an all-European legal threshold for the allowable amount of alcohol in the blood of drivers. Because here again, practical situations dictate the need for such co-operation. Anyone who has driven in Europe must marvel at the clarity of most road signs and their ability to transcend language differences with a few simple designs. And the number of people on the road makes it obvious that even the drinking habits of drivers have to be harmonized, lest a person who had a perfectly legitimate half bottle of wine with his lunch near the French border should be arrested as a drunk driver only a few kilometers away.

The Commission of the European Community has also been unifying the standards for vehicles. First there were uniform specifications for rear license plates and bumpers, then for horns and rearview mirrors. Next came a requirement for dual brakes, spare parts bearing the EEC stamp of approval, maximum noise and exhaust pollution levels, safety glass, and other forms of passenger protection. Obviously, the fact that so many cars are constantly being used in countries outside their place of manufacture or registration makes it imperative that such standards be about the same—unless they are to be abandoned altogether. While it is easy to see the need for these unifying moves, it requires a little extra thought to envision all the proliferating results. Think how many companies are affected by all this; any auto-manufacturing company—including a US subsidiary—that is producing cars in Belgium or France or England must now be sure that its products conform to a continent-wide set of standards. And as this always means meeting the requirements of the most exacting nation, the end result is a car with stouter parts, more accessories, and a higher price tag. This involves more factory equipment, more bank financing to pay for the cars, higher insurance premiums, and so on. The travel industry's vulnerability to sudden cutbacks only serves to underscore the dynamic nature of a new market like Europe's. For if car production lags, it is not only auto factories and workers that feel the effect, but also laborers and investors in scores of related lines. The vested interests that develop in a burgeoning consumer market are far greater than in so many separate nations.

7

But Old Jealousies Pull Europe Apart

For each of the forces that tends to unify Europe there is a lively *but*—often with massive implications for the US and its business interests. Even before the fuel-supplying nations began a conscious drive to divide the Europeans, these contradictions were at work. Otherwise, no outside wedge could have found its way into the EEC.

Europe is supposed to become a new nation. *But* most people are unready to renounce their old allegiances. Even the youth who profess to care little for their own flags show no sign of a new European patriotism.

Everybody wants to travel in neighbor countries. *But* tourists have little effect on the desire for political unity. In practice, they are more apt to create irritation than fraternal feelings.

Freedom to own property anywhere in the Community is extolled. *But* the people of each country dislike any concentration of foreign ownership in their midst.

There is talk of blending languages and publications. *But* the attempts to do it in real life are few and of minor significance.

Education is aimed at leveling the frontiers. *But* the numbers who study outside their own country are trifling.

And educational accreditation from one country is seldom recognized in another.

Labor presses for equal conditions. *But* laborers in each country are hostile to immigrants. Moreover, union demands are already frightening some companies away from investments in parts of Europe.

Many of these are largely emotional reactions and insufficient to scuttle the unification program. There are other and stronger negative factors which will be assessed in the next few chapters. But emotions, enthusiasm, and apathy can make a vast difference in what happens at polling places and what the elected officials will feel impelled to do. So it is important to distinguish between the practicalities that pull Europeans together and the thought patterns that pry them apart.

France's late President Georges Pompidou learned about the lack of enthusiasm for Europe as a nation in a very painful way. In 1972, just before Britain's membership in the EEC was to be decided, Pompidou thought he would strengthen his own hand at upcoming summit talks and prove himself to be Europe's No. 1 leader by holding a referendum. The French people were asked to vote their approval of an expanded Common Market. The vote turned out to be limply affirmative; but instead of the burst of popular support that Pompidou had envisioned as a loud hurrah for his own leadership, the balloting was meager and decidedly spiritless. This in a nation that was prospering, that was getting its own way in most EEC disputes, and whose farmers were winning wider markets due to EEC policies.

Considering the poor response for so gentle an issue as expansion of economic co-operation, experts who study public opinion estimate that any vote on a proposal to merge the nations in a real sense and dissolve the old nationalities would lose by at least five to one. And there are some who believe that violent disorders might even prevent such a referendum. There is, in fact, virtually no real enthusiasm on the part of individuals for a new European nation; on the other hand, there may well be a strong undercurrent of the old patriotism for each separate country —needing only the appearance of a threat to spark it into flame.

The Commission in Brussels carefully refers to the separate members as "states" rather than "nations." Although the term technically covers any sovereign entity and is commonly used even in treaties between very distant countries, in Brussels it has the ambiguous merit of also making each member country sound like a mere local government within a federation, as in the USA. The Commission can and will hammer away at this note, but so far it seems to be outside the auditory range of the European public. The overwhelming majority of the continent's people think of themselves as French, German, Italian, et cetera. Any break in that pattern is a minifying, not a magnifying, one. Some citizens of France insist that they are really Breton or Basque; some who live in Belgium think themselves primarily Flemish or Walloon. Only a few intellectuals would insist on being called Europeans.

The remarks that are made about Germans outside their own boundaries, or the pained expressions that often take the place of remarks, are enough to demonstrate how divisive a factor success itself can be. Most often, it is not old wartime hatreds but new tourist irritations that underlie this. Memories are short and plastic, and many Europeans will say in confidence to a friend that German troops who occupied their town were better behaved and more respectful of the local wine cellars than the Americans who came in to supplant them. But today's busload of German tourists who stomp loudly through the art galleries are a much clearer annoyance. Naturally enough, the country with the heaviest employment turns out more tourists per capita, meaning more uncultured tourists who never traveled before. And so the "ugly German" is no more looked on as a compatriot than the Americans who started coming over in the 1950's.

When they buy up tracts of real estate in the most desirable beach and resort areas of nearby countries, the Germans again stir up animosities. Some nations outside the Community, such as Switzerland and Sweden, curb this by law. The EEC countries can't very well do that among themselves. So the Germans can put their enormous earnings to work in land and property, but they can't make the local people enthusiastic about it.

The long history of difference among Europeans makes this very natural. The obvious language barrier would, in itself, be enough to make the unification of Europe a very different task from the building of the American republic. Apart from people in the travel industry, only a very thin upper crust can easily communicate across all frontiers. Four great newspapers—*The Times* of London, *Le Monde* of Paris, Germany's *Die Welt,* and Italy's *La Stampa*—have joined to publish a tabloid supplement called *Europe* that appears in all four papers and reaches some five million readers. But the fact that it will focus on business news shows how restricted and special its readership will really be.

Despite the talk of co-ordinating education, there are some professions that are strictly sectioned according to countries. Medicine is the most determinedly national. Even little Luxembourg refuses to recognize anyone with a medical degree from any university other than its own. There is virtually no exchange of doctors or medical researchers among the member countries. Each country's physicians are sure that they are the best. And the people, who get used to certain health habits, are inclined to agree. An Englishman who finds that a French hospital serves wine to patients or that a Belgian hospital soothes babies with light beer can easily be convinced that medicine on the continent is primitive.

Even religious convictions can work against Europeanization. The Protestant-Catholic issue would, in fact, be playing a major part in the question of unification, were it not for the relative lassitude of religious feelings in our era. But even as it is, there are those who insist that the EEC is primarily a Papal stratagem to win supremacy for the Roman Church. No doubt the fact that it was founded by the Treaty of Rome abets their arguments. As one extremist tract published in England during the debate over entry into the EEC put it, "The Archbishop of Canterbury supports Britain's entry into the Common Market and doubtless he envisages a united Europe as a big ecumenical step towards reunion with Rome, on which his heart appears to be fixed." Since Pope Pius II is said to have coined the term "European" over five hundred years ago, the fact that Pius XII later urged Roman Catholics to support European unity is cited as evidence that this is part of a continuing plot to expand the Roman Church. Some four-fifths of the population of the original six EEC nations were Roman Catholics. So it is clear that what Britain, Ireland, and Denmark joined in 1973 was bound to be called (one Vatican official is said to have actually used the term) "the greatest Catholic super state the world has ever known," although the effect of thus diluting the proportion who are of that faith is seldom referred to.

. . .

But there is a type of negative feeling that is far more tangible and widespread than any of these emotions. And again it is the reverse side of a coin that we have already examined: labor, so vocal in the mass about equalizing the conditions of work all over Europe, consists largely of individuals who don't at all welcome an influx of strangers. In no other field is the word "foreigner" so much alive as in the meeting of local workers with migrants. At best, they are ostracized and viewed askance. At worst, they are beaten or even murdered.

· In Germany many workers must live in company dormitories, with house rules that are described as "suited to Victorian girls' schools." The lucky ones who can find homes for their families, according to a recent study, live in ancient buildings and pay thirty per cent more than the German average while getting much less space. And this in a country that is trying harder than most others to give migrant workers a fair break.

· A Yugoslav worker who fled from such conditions in Germany finds himself much worse off in Belgium. Having no work permit, he labors in a plastics factory at less than half the normal wage. The owner holds his passport, and now he can neither leave nor complain to the tough Belgian police.

· In Grasse, France, local vigilantes have conducted nightly raids on the immigrant quarter. And near Marseilles an Algerian shantytown was machine-gunned and a Molotov cocktail was thrown into a migrant worker's apartment.

Maybe it will eventually prove to be a good thing that Europeans are being forced to realize their own racist and xenophobic leanings. Until a few years ago there was unthinking criticism of Americans for their handling of a color problem that could not even be clearly visualized in the Old World. Without troubling to learn that the earnings, living standards, and educational opportunities of most blacks in the US far exceeded those of most whites in Europe, people abroad assumed that Americans had a vicious streak that was unknown to Europeans. Then it began to be seen that a much smaller concentration of blacks in Britain brought out violent antagonisms. The highly respected Swiss showed a determination to reduce the number of Italian workers in their midst, even at the cost of slowing their economy. And even within a single country, Italy, the flow of workers from south to north produced extreme dislike. In a few such cases, it is fair to say that some justification existed. A country like Switzerland could easily see its whole character change if it let a fourth or more of its population be composed of a foreign element; whatever we might think about the freedom of migrant workers, the right of Switzerland to remain essentially Swiss has not yet been contested. Similarly, the people of Milan or Turin have a point when they are appalled at a huge rise in violence and street crimes caused by new families from the south.

In some cases, however, the cause seems to be less reasonable and more emotional. In countries with absolutely full employment, where no jobs are threatened, local workers have been known to react against foreigners as though they were taking the bread from their mouths. In the usually sensible Netherlands, reaction against Turkish migrant workers reached the point where a number of Turks were killed. Since these emotions often break out where the incoming foreigners are taking only menial jobs that the local people no longer want to do, it has to be construed as a manifestation of the clannishness that is a built-in part of human nature. Perhaps it is a vestigial part, no longer needed, of the instinct to keep the tribe intact and safe from predators. But it does exist. And the very deep nationalism that goes with it cannot be ruled out of any assessment of Europe's chance for unity.

Labor also poses a threat to Europe's future because of its strong leftward lean. The huge new Confederation of Syndicates that bands together workers from fourteen countries has a strong vein of antagonism to capital and management. At the founding meeting, for instance, Germany's top labor leader said, "British colleagues, we don't need you at a distance. We want the wholehearted participation of your political and union strength." But a British leader, admitting that his country's workers had opposed joining the Common Market, explained why they mistrusted the EEC. They believe it favors big business—and especially multinational companies—to the detriment of the workers' interests. Therein lies one issue that could precipitate a deadly encounter. For some spokesmen have described the new body as "an international counterforce against the world-wide concentration of capital and its influence on European economic integration."

Note the ominous intimation of a class struggle. Free trade unions have everything to lose from any swing too far to the left. For an authoritarian government—communist or fascist—spells the end of free labor and collective bargaining. America's AFL-CIO knows this and fights communism as hard as any right-wing organization. But some very extreme elements within European labor seem oblivious to it. They even endorse the keen desire of Soviet and satellite trade unions to join the new West European labor confederation. So it is entirely possible that the unions will go beyond merely "countering" the concentration of capital and will make capital feel that new investments are undesirable. Or labor might push its demands to the point where even the workers tire of strikes and inflation, and welcome the coming of military coups. The more statesmanlike labor leaders know this, but cannot always control their own followers.

The Confederation presently speaks of "co-ordinating unions' responses to multinational companies, and working out joint views on manpower planning, social and economic policies, and worker participation." But in plain language this means the possibility of strikes that spread across the whole continent—of workers in thirteen countries ganging up to force a settlement in some industry in the fourteenth country. Why should they? Because they might feel that lower wages in a single neighbor nation threaten the jobs of all the rest. Or, in the positive sense, that increased pay or benefits in that other country will lead to higher standards for all. And one form of increase—"worker participation"—has already made many companies wonder about the wisdom of planning to expand in Europe; for they see it only as a euphemism for handing over their assets to the workers, and hence the death of the free-enterprise system.

Could anything more boldly underscore how great is America's stake in the course of European affairs? The labor factor alone—and there are other equally dangerous ones—could wreck the Old World's position as a great and free buffer against communism. It could make Europe the graveyard of many American subsidiaries, billions of dollars in American-owned stock, and all America's hopes for a Free World alliance to safeguard peace.

8

Money—the Greatest Problem

Unifying Europe's currencies into a single unit of exchange is the most elusive goal of all—and one of the most meaningful to the US. In no other field has the EEC made so many premature starts and achieved so little. For no other subject touches so many people and is understood by so few.

Money is a symbol of nearly everything in a society. To freeze all the separate currencies together, one would have to strait-jacket all the other policies—wages, fringe benefits, welfare, urban development, business expansion or contraction, tourism, investment, stock-market operations. Succeed in doing that and you have virtually united the nations.

The reason is this: in any geographical region, some areas are always more prosperous than others. The people who inhabit the richer areas want to keep their money to themselves and even to stay politically separate from the poorer parts, except perhaps to exploit the labor or the products of that neighboring land. This is not necessarily reprehensible; it is the principle of profit-making on which just about every human advance has been based. On the other hand, the people who live in less wealthy areas naturally want to improve their lot. So if they get into a political union with the richer neighbors, their representatives in the government will suggest tax and spending plans that draw money from the rich and distribute it to the poor. And as the poor usually seem to be more numerous, they wield increasing political power, and the flow of money tends to narrow the economic gap between the areas.

As long as nations have separate currencies, their periodic solution for the imbalance between wealthy and poor areas is to change the exchange rates between the various monies. The less prosperous nation keeps devaluing its currency, so that its products will sell more easily in other countries and fewer foreign goods will be imported. This does not equalize the areas; it merely makes it possible to balance accounts between them. But if those nations merge their currencies, a change in rates is ruled out. What would then become *regional* imbalances within a single nation would be offset by diverting income from more developed regions to the poorer ones. Taxes in the rich areas would be more than the public expenditures there, while the backward regions would get more public funds than they paid in taxes. Once that process begins, the political forces tend to continue it. And that is just why it is so hard to get agreement on a common currency.

Despite that, the EEC has made courageous sounds about working toward monetary union. As early as 1964 the EEC Council agreed that the member states were to consult before making any changes in the value of their currencies. And although there were a number of unilateral parity changes after that, the nations did always discuss them with each other in advance.

Political leaders, often with too little comprehension of monetary matters, made even greater promises for the sake of appearing to pull together against new American attitudes that had shaken them all. "From August 1971 on," as EEC Commissioner Ralf Dahrendorf sees it, "the US monetary moves highlighted the frightening transitional changes that made America and Europe no longer the kind of Senior-Junior partners they had been since World War II." But the promises to combine against this and make Europe's money independent of America often were ones they could not keep. At one point the nations actually agreed to co-ordinate their internal economic policies and to narrow the amount of fluctuations between their currencies. Without going into the technical complexities of their agreements, it is helpful to understand that they set narrower limits for the fluctuation among their monies than the range that applied among other countries. Later, when a system of "floating" rates permitted other currencies to move in relation to each other without a set limit, most of the EEC countries still tried to hold the rates among themselves within a fairly narrow range. But note the words "most of." Italy and Britain were exempted from the original agreement, showing that the task of locking together regions with the most marked differences in affluence was not yet feasible. Even before this, there had been an admission that the bold words of agreement were unwise, because Italy had very naturally reneged on the general promise that each member nation would settle its accounts with the others partly in gold. Italy, which had heavy debts to some of its neighbors at the end of each quarter, refused to give up any gold at the low "official price" then prevailing. Rather than precipitate a showdown, the other nations agreed to put off the settlements. When France also cut loose from the monetary tie in 1974, the whole attempt had to be dropped. And further attempts at interim co-operation and a patchwork policy on gold have only reinforced the impression that real monetary unity is far off.

All these were different aspects of the one central fact that governments in the post-World War II era became increasingly unwilling to face any kind of harsh economic truths. "To achieve high employment levels without devaluation or price stability without revaluation" was—as an EEC release admitted—just as much the goal in Brussels as in any other capital of the modern world. But that apparently laudable aim conflicts with natural laws and with arithmetic. High employment levels mean, for one thing, tremendously multiplied consumption of raw materials. Those supplies come from other nations. The hectic competition for such limited materials *must* drive the prices skyward. And paying for them, while also paying far higher wages to the labor force at home, is bound to distort the relative values of a nation's products. This has to mean devaluations and revaluations. That is another way of saying that nations must keep breaking their word—to other governments and to their own citizens who hold currency. And no long-term good has ever come from irresponsibility and deception.

The EEC governments must, in all justice, be said to be partly the victims of a US attitude that made good money management in Europe all but impossible. The American insistence on escaping from the discipline of gold and mismanaging the US economy had sent inflationary tidal waves across the Atlantic. Some hundred billion dollars had surged over to Europe, the result of free spending and investing of an unprecedented sort. It would have taken considerable heroism abroad to resist the trend. The Europeans would have had to agree among themselves on a new price for gold and new gold-based values for their own currencies, then raise their currencies in value relative to the dollar—in effect devaluing the US dollar indirectly. That would have halted the flow, but also the easy profits.

Instead, they allowed bad practices to go on, because they were helping to keep a boom going in Europe. And so they wound up with that old, old European condition in which gold and land come to seem the only reliable assets and are bid up to staggering prices.

Now the dollar problem and Europe's own currency instability are inextricably entwined. The question of how to deal with America's debt stands in the way of every attempt to calm Europe's money markets. Sometimes, in fact, the US currency gets caught up in purely European situations and is made to seem either weaker or stronger than it is. Every time there is some imbalance between pounds and marks or francs and lira, the government that moves in to support one of those currencies is likely to use dollars for the transaction. A central bank that wants to buy British pounds, for example, is apt to buy them with American dollars, because that is what everyone has the most of. This use of the dollar as an "intervention currency" simply means that stacks of them often are dumped onto the money markets almost by accident. At other times a government that would like to sell off dollars is afraid of depressing the dollar's value, which could hurt its own foreign trade. So the dollars are held and made to seem stronger than they really are. And, of late, Europe's shortage of cash to pay for petroleum imports has led it to use billions of its dollar holdings for the purpose. This also gives an impression of dollar strength. But the Mideast countries that become the new owners of this currency will eventually demand something in return, for the dollars are still an obligation of the USA. Of course, none of this could happen if there were not far too many dollars outstanding overseas. And what is to be done about them?

Washington's perennial request to Europe has seemed reasonable enough: "Let us sell you more of our goods while you restrain your sales to us, and in that way we'll earn enough to reduce the debt." But the European response has been equally logical: "That would wreck our society. You are asking us to use your products and to make less of our own—throwing millions of people out of work. Governments would fall, and we would move sharply to the left. Everything you once did to save us from communism would be lost."

Finding no good answer to that, Washington tells Europe and other dollar holders abroad to keep the money or invest it in American securities and earn a return on it. But both parties know that such interest earned will only keep increasing the debt. There have been times recently when large US farm exports and the odd effects of the energy crisis have made the dollar look healthier. But that is a cruel deception. It would take well over a decade of consecutive and massive US trade surpluses to bring the overhang of dollars abroad down to reasonable proportions; and that would shatter the economies of Europe and Japan. The potential bitterness this subject could rouse is indicated by the snide jest that the US has already collected large war reparations from Germany by repeatedly devaluing the dollars that reposed in Germany's treasury.

And so this imported problem fuels more and more inflation in Europe and aggravates the mountainous task of stabilizing the EEC's own currencies. Looking ahead to the start of the 1980's, it seems highly unlikely that European governments will find acceptable formulas for uniting their monies.

Many men who know the workings of the money markets are among the most skeptical. They could be wrong—overly absorbed in the technical problems. But they cannot be ignored. "European monetary co-operation is a paper tiger," comments Managing Director C. F. Karsten, of the

Amsterdam-Rotterdam Bank, N.V. "It won't work because most of the devices, such as the narrower range of fluctuation, only make it possible for speculators to gamble on parity changes with even less risk. Moreover, it can't work because member governments can run balance-of-payments deficits with impunity. There are no real sanctions to enforce the rules."

Nonetheless, the sweeping promises continue to be made. One EEC summit meeting reaffirmed the "determination of the enlarged Community irreversibly to achieve economic and monetary union." In 1973 the European Monetary Co-operation Fund, headquartered in Luxembourg, began operations; this was like setting up a central bank for the European Community.

What more could anyone expect of countries that had so recently been entirely separate? Nothing more, and actually quite a lot less. But the fact that what is being tried is remarkable need not force us to accept every glowing forecast of what more is to come. The sacrifices that would have to be made by certain governments—especially Germany, the Low Countries, and France—in order to achieve real monetary union are huge. Some, like Belgium, the Netherlands, and Luxembourg, might be willing to go along in return for the chief aim of complete political integration that they have always favored. Being small, each of them sees its highest destiny as part of a great new nation. Germany might possibly have agreed to this some years ago, before her officials in Bonn began to tire of being so acquiescent to the others. But even if no other nation balked, France would surely draw the line at such a surrender of national sovereignty. "Only if she won her own way on every point—the location, rules, and future policies of the EEC's monetary program—would France consider allowing it to become a reality," one prominent European told me.

"And even in that case, I somewhat doubt it. These promises to work toward brilliant future goals seem more to me like short-term maneuvers to appear co-operative while actually planning ways to scuttle the whole program long before it comes to anything."

9

There Is No *European Foreign Policy*

One other good measure of the EEC's movement toward nationhood is this: how much of a concerted foreign policy toward the rest of the world has it been able to agree on?

For it is *foreign* policy that makes a true nation. There are areas, political units, in South Asia and Africa, for example, that govern themselves, yet are not sovereign states because a government in New Delhi or Johannesburg conducts all their relations with foreign powers. Much more than mere prestige is involved in this. Only if a government has charge of its external affairs can it be sure that its domestic plans will not be altered by outside interference.

In the case of the European Community there is hardly any more harmony on foreign policy than there was among the separate nations of a quarter-century ago. Each of the nine countries retains its own mission to the United Nations, and there is no tendency to concert their approaches to major issues.

A dramatic demonstration of this occurred in 1972, when the UN Commission on Trade and Development had a global meeting in Chile. It was the moment for the modern countries to meet with the developing ones and talk of the help they planned to extend. "But it proved to be a terrible experience for any of us who want to see Europe really amount to something," recalls a dedicated member of the EEC's ruling Commission. "There we were with our first chance to act like a *nation,* to present a common front to the rest of the world. And the EEC came with *no policy or program at all.* It was just the time for saying, 'Here is what the European Community proposes for the developing nations.' Instead, each man from the EEC spoke as a Belgian or a Netherlander or a Frenchman, and each one told what *his* country proposed to do."

As on other subjects, there are minor concessions and compromises. A member of the ruling Council of Ministers confided to me, for example, that an apparent disagreement over when and how to recognize the new state of Bangladesh was actually a neatly turned plan among the European governments. All nine members had decided on recognition; but some wanted to appear eager, and others saw an advantage in seeming reluctant. Britain insisted on being first, in order to please the Indians, who had supported separatism for Bangladesh. France, on the other hand, wanted to appear loath to recognize the carving up of land that had belonged to Moslem Pakistan, in line with its policy of playing up to the Arab countries. Once it was decided that Britain would announce recognition first and France would wait until last, the other seven nations rather easily compromised on the order in which each one would issue its public statement.

It is also true that there is general agreement among the EEC members, and even the other European countries, on the greatest single foreign issue that nations can have—territorial ambition. As of now, such a drive is surely at the lowest point that it has ever been. Save for the unresolved separation of the German people, we could say that territorial ambition in Western Europe is dead. The fact that so many capitals, after long regarding each other as aggressors or victims, now have no thought of paring away a neighbor's land is very significant. The new attitude may derive, in part, from the ascendance of industry over agriculture, so that now manpower and resources become more important than land. And since territory has always been one of the chief causes of war, the lack of hunger for it and the absolute feeling against any more European wars must be seen as one kind of general agreement on foreign policy. It is not proof that there will be no future turn back toward territorial disputes, but it certainly demonstrates a big change from the past.

And there is still another foreign policy subject on which most of Europe might be said to agree—anticolonialism. No EEC government would think of raising a voice in favor of permanent ownership of overseas territories. A cynic is free to believe that this is hypocritical. It started with the fear that communist countries would otherwise gain points in the less developed world; later it became a fad that forced even the greatest colonial powers to talk as though their past had been sinful. The same cynic might also inquire how nations that today declare themselves so much in favor of developing the poorer countries can be so disgusted by the colonial period that laid the foundation for such development. But sincere or not, there is no doubt that Europe generally "agrees" on noncolonialism. Even the French and British are forced to pretend that the developing areas in which they are predominant are merely business partners, as in some respects they are.

But does France allow Germany or Italy to become entirely an equal in trading with former French territories of Africa? Does Belgium pretend that the former Congo is equally open to all European business interests? No; it would be impractical, for one thing. Long relationships leave business ties that cannot be duplicated by others. And more importantly, each nation wants very much to nurture its own assets and gain even more of them.

When a high Belgian official visited Leopoldville several years after the uprisings of the Lumumba era, the local people lined up joyfully along the route of his motorcade, and there were cries of "Hurray! The Belgians are back!" They are, indeed. They never really left. Belgium directs much more foreign-aid money to the area that was once the Congo. And along with it goes commercial investment and a considerable amount of specialized personnel. Some neighborhoods of the capital city are heavily peopled with Belgians—administrators, bankers, technicians. They are needed to help run the country, and the local population is glad to see a part of the old relationship intact. Italy has a similar foothold in Libya. The rancor of postcolonial days is largely forgotten; even people who once were antagonists—or whose parents were—feel more akin to each other than they do to total strangers. So when the Khaddafy government, for all its radical aggressiveness, found that it must deal with Europe, it moved largely through Italian business channels. When huge numbers of oil dollars were to be converted into gold or German marks, the Libyans placed their orders through Italian bankers. Each nation of the Community finds that the laws of business and nature assist its resolve to preserve and expand its old stakes in other lands.

Therein lies the key to why there is no concerted external policy in Brussels. Each country is most anxious to make further headway *on its own* in the world race for influence, power, resources, money. It is perfectly natural; but it is the natural behavior of separate countries, not of states in a union.

. . .

Gaston Thorn, Luxembourg's foreign minister, pointed out to me a seldom-noticed fact that emphasizes Europe's division in foreign affairs. "When you hear it said that difficult negotiations and disputes on many issues lie ahead between Europe and America, note carefully that this means between the EEC *as a whole* and America," Thorne reminds. "But be sure to realize that there are no important differences between most of the individual governments of Europe and the government in Washington. Most of us separately get along fine with the USA. Only when we try to deal as a group do we run into trouble."

Of the several interpretations that could be given to this fact, the likeliest is that Brussels' difficulties with other capitals result largely from the complexity of merging many shades of opinion—in short, from disarray, rather than from policy—and that the separate national aims of each member government make this disarray unresolvable. Each member nation could get along with Washington, let us say, but only by making its own concessions in order to get its own goals in return. As soon as it suggests such concessions for the whole EEC, six or eight other countries will complain that they would be badly affected. And so neither the separate states nor the EEC as a whole can bargain freely. Each member government clings to just enough of its old prerogatives to prevent any truly independent foreign policy—either at the national or the supranational level.

Subconsciously, there is a reason even deeper than money and trade that prevents the separate nations from entrusting their destinies to a central EEC government: it is the lack of a true European defense force. Never before in political history has a "nation" as potentially important as Europe been almost totally reliant on another—and distant—power for its own protection. Great-power status may or may not involve a responsibility for the defense of others; it is nonsense to pretend to it without even the means of *self*-defense. The only near parallel also belongs to our own distorted era: Japan became a major industrial and commercial power while relying on the US for protection. But that was a calculated effort to avoid needless expense at a time when armed forces could only have been a burden. There is little doubt that Japan has the unity, the capacity, and the intention of quickly becoming a military power again whenever the Asian power balance makes it desirable. Europe lacks the first of those requisites—the unity. And so its various capitals have a sense of insecurity and very differing views on where to look for their safety. Some of them look to a stand-off between the superpowers that would allow Europe to be an oasis of peace. Others frankly look to America as the chief support. And all of them acknowledge that American power is the crucial factor that makes Russia stay out of Western Europe. Not even the French, with their self-reliant attitude and their independent little hoard of nuclear bombs, pretend that they would have much deterrent effect if there were no America in the background.

Thus the technology of this century has decreed that a community of peoples striving to come together as one of the most populous, most productive, and richest nations on earth are destined not to be masters in their own house. Although nearly ninety per cent of NATO forces now are European, they are only the tripwire, designed to stall a Russian advance just long enough to let Washington make its move. Any European who looks deeply into the situation sees that the ultimate sovereign power—the power of life and death—is in America. Even those who look only at the surface cannot help noticing that such a major item of modern power as the big transport airplane comes to Europe from America. The Franco-British co-operation on the Concorde was remarkable, but more for its uniqueness than for its significance in the air lanes. All those European airlines competing with each other and advertising their great features are flying mostly American 707's or 747's. Subconsciously, no European can fail to know what that would mean if translated into terms of military air transport and striking power. And that, in a deep psychological sense, stands as a barrier against any feeling of real nationhood.

All times in history have been shot through with contradictions. Few have had as many conflicts as our era. Everyone wants more buying power with less inflation, more cars with less congestion, more fuel with less pollution. And European politics is as confused as the rest. The people of the old continent want independence without self-reliance. They want to be free of American influence while looking to Washington for their ultimate security.

10

The Non-members and Their Future

So central to world affairs has the European Community become that the term "non-member" is now the standard way of referring to any of the other countries around it. Say "non-member" in a gathering of diplomats and most of them—even without knowing the subject under discussion—will assume that you mean a non-member of the *EEC*. This is due not only to the size of the Community, but also to the peripheral nature of the rest of Europe. There are as many nations outside as in; but they are far smaller, less populous, and scattered around the edges of the great nine-member group.

Norway, Sweden, Finland, Austria, Spain, Portugal, Greece, Yugoslavia, and Switzerland are the main countries now trying to accommodate themselves to life with a giant that aspires to become the United States of Europe. Like the Canadians in relation to the USA, they find the experience more than a little uncomfortable. And like Canada they cannot even have the hope that internal troubles will strike the neighbor and benefit them. For it is their main trading partner, and life with a distempered giant would be worst of all.

The relationship among these nations is of very serious

importance to the USA. It can affect our trade, our investments in Europe, and our defense posture there. For these non-EEC countries include NATO members (Norway, Portugal, and Greece), at least two important trading nations (Sweden and Austria), and a major monetary power (Switzerland).

The normal course of events would be for these smaller units to drift into membership with the Common Market, and perhaps two or three of them will. But the process will be slow and for some it will not come at all, because each of them has some special problem of its own that has barred joining.

Norway has been closest to outright membership. When England, Ireland, and Denmark joined, the Oslo government had also negotiated its way into the EEC, and only the formality of a national referendum in Norway remained. Many outsiders thought there was no doubt of the outcome, since Norway is largely dependent on trade with the EEC—which buys so many of Norway's ships and such a large part of its fish. But as referendum day approached, one of those surges of pure emotion that occasionally grip a nation caught hold of Norway. Irrational as it was, there is something exciting in the spectacle of a country old in history but only a separate state since 1905 summoning up a patriotism that defied economics. A bizarre coalition of farmers and fishing interests mounted a massive campaign to convince the people that their sovereignty was being surrendered. That fishermen should have been so ready to turn away from their best customers on the continent lent a touch of panache to the affair. And Norwegians living in the far north struck an even more historic note when, on the eve of the referendum, they lit huge bonfires that made Norway's whole northern horizon glow. This was the ancient Norse signal that a foreign invader was threatening. And on the following day the people of Norway voted "no" to the EEC by a stunning margin.

Because this is the twentieth century and political leaders think in terms of arranging commercially viable compromises rather than holding deadly grudges, the EEC soon arranged a special treaty with Norway, and trade—even if slightly jarred—did go on. But this was only after one Norwegian government had fallen in consternation at the ruin of its long negotiation. And so it is unlikely that any prime minister in Oslo will try his luck on the membership issue for quite some time to come. And the urgency of it has been diminished by an unexpected happening that may indicate the Almighty's wish to reward those who put principle above expediency: Norway turns out to be uniquely immune to the energy crisis that burst on Europe late in 1973. She is more nearly self-sufficient in fuel than those wealthier neighbors of the EEC. By early 1974 some investors on the continent were even shifting funds from EEC countries to Oslo! Norway remains the prime candidate to boost the EEC's membership to ten, but it is not likely to happen soon.

Neighboring Sweden is a much more complex case. The Swedes are highly practical, have less fear than any other nation of free-trade competition, and would have been among the first to align with the EEC if the Treaty of Rome meant nothing more than industry and commerce. But the Rome Treaty also implies a commitment to political co-operation—if not outright union. And it just happens that the Community is also the geographical heartland of NATO. Sweden's passion for neutrality is legendary, and so Stockholm has done no more than hint at the chance of joining with a special status—participation in all the trade and tariff arrangements, but with no political entanglements. The EEC members have been cool to this. Some of them are not too keen about seeing the highly efficient Swedes in anyway. This is the nation that was so coolly clinical some years ago as to cut its tariffs intentionally in order to kill off its inefficient industries. It worked, and the lagging plants and displaced workers were shifted into new lines that could compete better in the world. But a country that works that way can be an uncompromising partner, and so the European Community is not likely to bend its rules for the privilege of letting Sweden in.

On the other hand, Sweden may be forced to bend its own neutrality in order to ask admission. If problems in other parts of the world cause protectionist barriers to spring up, a country that relies on the export of industrial goods may find it harder and harder to sell if she is not inside one of the great blocs. And so Stockholm might be able to face the idea of living inside an EEC that is not really moving very fast toward nationhood. Especially if NATO continues to lose vitality and there is no insistence on Swedish adherence to the Western Alliance, the risk of offending Russia or one day being a target for Soviet missiles may be minimized.

Both Finland and Austria are very special cases that cannot possibly join the EEC under present conditions because the Soviet Union would not permit it. Both operate as parts of the Western capitalist system by Russia's leave. That is in the fine print of the arrangements they live by, and it is no discredit to either country. Austria, in fact, has made a few rather gallant gestures of defiance at times—such as making it plain that Russia's move into Czechoslovakia was abhorrent and receiving some Czech refugees. It suits Russia's convenience to have both these nations in an anomalous status between East and West; but neither of them could be allowed to swing all the way over.

Besides, Austria has an undercurrent of lingering ambition that is remarkable in so small a country. She has not at all forgotten that Vienna once ruled an Austro-Hungarian Empire that was vast, even if poorly knit. A quiet reservoir of monarchical sentiment still resides in many Austrian hearts. And the belief—probably mistaken—that neighboring parts of her old Empire still lean toward Austrian rule is very persistent. Soon after that Russian move into Czechoslovakia, for example, a trade fair was held at Poznan, and contingents from all the Soviet satellite countries were there. "As one delegation after another was introduced," an Austrian cabinet minister told me, "there was only the mildest applause. Then the name of Austria was mentioned, and there was a great cheer, and most of the audience rose to its feet. I felt then that they were all thinking how different it would be to be ruled by Vienna, rather than Moscow." The cheering probably was a sentimental recognition of Austria's courage in having opposed the Russian move, and nothing more. But the dream of someday becoming again the coalescing point for a whole group of neighbors—whom the Austrians feel they understand better than anyone else—prevents Vienna from wanting to be swallowed up by the EEC. Business, yes, as much as possible. But nothing more.

Spain, Portugal, Greece, and Yugoslavia are separated from membership by both material and ideological barriers. All are less developed and have lower per capita incomes than the Community's member countries. And all have authoritarian or uncertain governments. Oddly enough, this latter point is probably the less troublesome of the two, if the talk of membership should become serious. The global trend to government by dictator or military junta cannot be hidden. Note how many nations of Africa, Latin America, and Asia have leaped or slipped into such an arrangement, after experimenting with democracy. In many cases this has been due to a lack of trained civil servants, and the impossibility of putting together a representative government on short notice in the absence of a parliamentary tradition. In other cases, parliamentarism has degenerated into fragmentation. And whichever the case, the people have welcomed the imposition of something that at least resembles a government.

And so, when respectability no longer depends on being democratic, it is easy to envision further developments in Portugal, for example, that could remake its image neatly enough to convince Brussels of its acceptability. But economic readiness for membership is a much slower process.

For note what would happen if an underdeveloped country suddenly came into full membership: the country's farmers being smaller and less efficient producers, agricultural goods would have to be protected against imports from the other members. The country's relatively few factories would be new, small, and unaccustomed to the low-cost production of the major nations. They would be killed off by the outside competition unless they, too, were protected by special tariffs. So the incoming member would be asking for special favors at every turn, blocking the sales that other members might hope to make there; yet any of its industries that happen to be competitive with those of the outside would be allowed to sell in the rest of the Community with no tariffs imposed at the borders. So it is the other members, rather than the poorer country, that tend to shy away from accepting the less-developed country. Spain, therefore, is closest of this group to nearing the point of membership. The country's leadership seems anxious to bring Spain up to the level of industrialization that could make it a full member of Europe.

Finally, there is Switzerland—the one nation that is certain *not* to join the EEC. Even if they see themselves surrounded by a Europe that has melted entirely into one bloc, the Swiss will not give up their neutrality and their total sovereignty. They are a breed that carved a beautiful country out of solid rock, and they glory in their separateness. They have a remarkable ability to be open to other countries and other ideas, yet to be unaffected by them. And they are quite ready to slam the door in the face of any neighbor whose approach threatens the tranquility of the Swiss. Even to a greater degree than Sweden, Switzerland makes a dogma of her neutrality and of her right to do whatever suits the nation's best interests. As important a monetary power as she is, for instance, Switzerland does not belong to the International Monetary Fund and has refused to take part in commissions that work on monetary reform. They can come and meet in a Swiss city if they like, and the Swiss government tries to learn what was done in their meetings, for the sake of practical commercial intelligence. But to be bound by any agreement that might tell Switzerland what to do with her gold, her interest rates, or the exchange rate of the franc—this is unthinkable. So is the notion of membership in a Community that tries to standardize nearly everything.

The outlook, then, is for no increase in the basic membership of nine for the next several years. By the end of the seventies Norway may well approach the EEC again, and there is some chance that Sweden will follow. Only in the next decade is it likely that Spain and Greece might be economically ready to come in on a full basis. And the status of Finland and Austria—almost as if they were Soviet satellite nations—depends on the overall East-West relationship. But whether the EEC stays at nine members or moves to twelve, fourteen, or more, the magnetic attraction exerted by the heart of the continent is much the same. Even today, these countries that are included among the so-called "nonmembers" are, in fact, either "associate members" or have special treaties with the Community. Some of them do more two-way trading with the EEC than some of the full member nations. Austria and Norway, for example, do a much larger *proportion* of their total trade with the Community than England does.

And that is where the United States interest comes in. When the Community enlarged from six to nine members and when it then made special arrangements with the peripheral countries that did not join, the problem of selling US goods into those areas became still more difficult. American products that were narrowly competitive in Spain or Sweden before might now be beaten out by German items that pay a lower duty rate when they reach their destination.

From the time when the EEC's enlargement was announced, the US began to insist that its trade would be damaged. It asked for tariff concessions that would enable US goods to sell there at less of a disadvantage. "If Europe is still as dedicated to free trade as she claims to be," said Abe Katz, then the State Department's chief of Atlantic Economic Affairs, "it would be in order now for Brussels to do what it did in years past—grant a cut in tariffs on the products of America and other countries. That would prove that it is still 'outward-looking.' But a group that swaps discriminatory tariff concessions on the inside and uses them to discourage trade with the outside is near to becoming a protectionist state."

Part of the reason for Europe's reluctance to concede lay in its fear of Japan. Any tariff cut that is extended to a member of GATT (General Agreement on Tariffs and Trade) must also be given to all other GATT nations. So any concessions made to America apply equally to Japan. And the Europeans have an abnormal fear of Japan's ability to invade a market. Even when only a few per cent of Europe's imports were from Japan, these had seriously wounded two entire industries—stereo recorders in Germany, electronic calculators in Sweden—by focusing on a lucrative line, producing a high-quality product at a good value, then moving in with strong merchandising methods. All very legitimate, and not dissimilar from the tactics that European firms might use to capture a market in America, Canada, or Latin America. But to have the tactic used on them was unnerving. And so the Community's dealings with Japan have been tentative and stand-offish. Even when a Tokyo group comes to buy heavily, its aggressiveness arouses mixed feelings. And the awe in which Europeans hold the Japanese as sellers is more like the terror of a military invader than like a businessman's worry about a competitor.

Under a steady bombardment of American demands, Europe finally did give some concessions to offset the effects of EEC enlargement. But they were minor—more symbolic than practical—and they did not change the impression that the other great industrial and trading areas of the world are to be kept at arm's length. The ultimate question is: *in how many countries* will American and Japanese products face a disadvantage? How many more "nonmembers" will be woven into the network of nations that exchange preferential treatment with the EEC? For any increase beyond the present level may well cause America's reaction to rise from complaints to retaliations.

11

Europe as the East-West Buffer

Each man sees himself as the center of the world. So does each country—even the smallest. A wise government may be very humble and objective about its own importance in the global pattern, but it will not accept that as a reason for letting itself be used. It will, instead, examine each situation for ways of improving its position.

Knowing that, it should now seem absurd that West Europe should ever have been viewed as a permanent buffer between America and Russia. It did serve that purpose admirably for two decades, but only because Soviet policy had been clumsy. Caught in an ideological vise between communist grimness and American affluence, there could be no doubt about which way Europe would wish to lean. The arrangement worked well for both the US and Europe. It cost America billions of dollars to keep Europe protected—to fly Berlin airlifts, build bases, leave thousands of American soldiers abroad as semipermanent tourists symbolizing to both Europe and Russia that the American presence would not be violated or budged. Europe gained freedom from immediate fear and exemption from larger military outlays of its own. America gained a span of time when the Soviet ambition was held in check. And during that time,

Washington was practically the capital of Europe when it came to making global decisions. More than once, an especially compliant part of Europe, such as Britain or Germany, was referred to as "our fifty-first state."

That changed much more sharply than necessary when America caught the Southeast-Asian disease. Had Washington never let Europe feel second in importance, the foundations of the Atlantic Community need not have been shaken. But some adjustments in the mentality of the partnership would have been in order. No nation or region will go on thinking of itself as a buffer for long. Nor was that the natural way for Russia to see Europe.

Viewed from Moscow, Europe is a neighbor. It is not just a barrier between Russia and America, but a major entity in itself. Often, believe it or not, Europe has been seen as a menacing neighbor, because its affluence contrasted so sharply with the grayness of East Europe. But the contrast gradually became less stark and the advantages of dealing with Europe became more apparent to the USSR. Most significant of all, Russia became very adept at dealing with the nations of Europe as separate governments—playing on the fears and aspirations of each one. And for the sake of clear understanding, none of this should be seen as a nefarious communist plot. It is sensible, patriotic behavior by Russian statesmen, just as the Soviet determination not to be second in missiles or at sea is exactly what an American military man would strive for if he had been born Russian.

Still looking at it as if we were sitting in a Moscow office, the priority goal was to nail down Russia's hold on the satellite nations of Eastern Europe. What a worry those countries were! Czechs, Hungarians, Rumanians had a history of dealing closely with the Germans and Austrians. They tended to keep doing that regardless of iron curtains and border guards. You can't keep soldiers stretched across every open field in Europe. "Even at the worst moments of the Cold War, our people were steadily trading and bartering farm produce with those of Hungary and Rumania," an Austrian official told me. "Their families had been doing it for centuries. Borders are mainly in geography books. Land and people just flow on continuously." And the worst of it—still seen from Moscow—was that any relaxation of policy toward the West would increase this interchange to dangerous proportions. First Khrushchev and then his successors wanted very much to seem friendlier with the West, to gain from trade and also to soften the Western Alliance. But might it not soften the Soviet bloc instead?

The risk had to be taken, and so the Kremlin set out along two paths: one was to talk constantly of easing tensions between the East and West as *blocs*—to loosen the ties of fear between America and Europe and also among the separate states of Europe. The other was to start dealing with two key nations of Europe as separate powers. It was easy to do that with France, for Charles de Gaulle was its chief, and he was born to be a separate power. So Moscow pretended to understand and sympathize with De Gaulle's vision of one Europe from the Atlantic to the Urals, well knowing that it was just a figure of speech and a way of throwing dust in the eyes of the pro-Americans. Khrushchev went to Paris and other Soviet leaders later followed him, and De Gaulle threw the NATO headquarters out of France. The French even sided with Russia on some key issues, being roughly of the same opinion in the Mideast and on Vietnam. But De Gaulle was never for a moment budged from his own goals; he was using Russia to advance the separate identity of France. The Soviets knew it. But they willingly went along because it was the gambit that allowed them to move on their real objective—West Germany.

If Bonn could be made to deal separately with Moscow, how that would shake up the Western Alliance! The principle of acting as a group, of never having side conversations with the great rival, was one of the foundations of the Western Alliance. And the Germans were NATO's most loyal members. They knew themselves to be the one European nation that Russia and its satellites really hated and feared; they willingly put more than their share of money and troops into NATO; and they were as staunch about German-American relations as John F. Kennedy had been when he told the ecstatic crowd of Berliners, "You are our brothers!" How could the Kremlin induce these Germans to talk privately with them? The ground was prepared by means of the contacts with France. Germany and France, hard as they tried to be close partners within the EEC, were such old rivals that the Moscow-Paris relationship had to cause Bonn policymakers some sleepless nights. And this set the stage for a bizarre incident when Hans Kroll, Bonn's ambassador in Moscow, had hours of long talks with Khrushchev about Russo-German relations. Not Russo-NATO, but strictly on the *bilateral* aspect. When the word of this leaked out, the ambassador was recalled and Bonn pretended that he had acted improperly on his own. Washington knew that wasn't so—that he had Adenauer's blessing—but accepted the explanation, since it had no legal right to control Bonn's actions. Washington also knew, then, that the brotherhood was in for rough times. This became more evident in the mid 1960's when Willy Brandt, still mayor of Berlin, dealt directly with several leading Russian officials, even though the Erhard government was not directly involved. Separate talks, promises, deals would become more and more the way of life.

And although the theme was muted while the Christian Democrats continued to govern Germany, it was loudly trumpeted from the day that Willy Brandt gained enough power to act entirely on his own. The Brandt *Ostpolitik,* or Eastern policy, was openly in favor of separate negotiations with Moscow and with each East European nation on strictly bilateral issues, while it still insisted that Germany was a dedicated member of the Western Alliance when it came to bloc relations. It was true. Brandt made historic breakthroughs in dealing with the formerly intransigent East Germans. He made a great concession to Poland on an old frontier issue. He made a major agreement with Moscow on the status of Berlin. Some of these moves seem to have been unwise, giving Russia more than she gave, firming her hold on the East, and perhaps further weakening the status of Berlin. But it was entirely true that the very pro-American Brandt discussed them with Washington and tried to make sure that they did not violate any NATO principles.

What they *did* shatter completely was the tradition that the Western allies must speak with only one voice—and in an American accent. If Germany could deal separately with Moscow, so could The Hague and Brussels and Rome. They did. Brezhnev came to summit meetings in each capital. Italian companies concluded huge deals to construct factories in Russia, making a mockery of US attempts to slow down Russia's growth in some strategic lines. And inevitably Washington's separate talks with Moscow became more intense—and were watched more jealously by the others.

The Washington-Moscow summitry was of long standing, of course, going back before the German moves. Some observers even feel that early meetings—such as Lyndon Johnson's Glassboro talks with Aleksei Kosygin—were the real start of the "separatist" movement. But Europeans seldom suspected in those years that Washington might be acting against *their* interests when it talked to Moscow. Most of them welcomed the summit meetings, for they regarded themselves as the potential battlefield on which tensions might be fought out; any détente was a relief. But when Europeans themselves began talking directly to Moscow, it somehow made them much more suspicious of Washington's motives. As soon as "every man for himself" becomes the rule, everyone's actions are eyed askance.

At that point, Russia made another move to induce even greater disarray among the Western powers. She called for a "European Security Conference," which all European nations would attend. Nobody knew what that was supposed to mean. European security had always been thought of as "security against Russia." Now the devil was suggesting that "we all have an ecumenical meeting and decide what to do about sin." It took many months for the West to know how to react. Italy's Manlio Brosio, having just resigned as Secretary-General of NATO, took on the special job of trying to decipher Russia's intentions. Security against China was one possible explanation. But no one seriously believed that so huge a conference was needed to talk solely about the distant threat of Chinese aggression. The best guess was that Russia, once again, was mainly trying to nail down its own hold on East Europe. It was trying to make the present borders unchangeable, to ensure that trade and interchanges between East and West Europe could take place without any fancy notions such as Czechoslovakia's Dubček once had of making a satellite country more Western than Eastern.

China did enter into Russia's reasons, as the "second front" that could best be dealt with only when the USSR was sure of its Western front. The fear that some satellites might seize the chance to flee to the West if Russia got embroiled with China could be eased by a complete understanding on "European security." For this reason, China bitterly resented the security conference. A strong NATO caused Russia to keep heavy troop concentrations on her Western front. Any mutual reduction in this area would free more Soviet forces for duty on the Russo-Chinese border. The leader of a Peking delegation said to a high NATO official in a private talk, "Why do you want to negotiate with those Russians? If you knew those devils as we know them, you would realize how fruitless negotiation is." And one of the small group of Asian experts that accompanied President Nixon and Henry Kissinger on the historic trip to Peking recalled to me an incident that took place during a meeting with Chou En-lai. The Chinese leader said that there was no reason for US troops to be stationed outside their own country. And he added, "Our discussion should include the general aim of bringing them all back to your own shores." To which a quick-witted member of the American contingent replied, "Anything is worth discussing. Shall we start by talking about bringing home the American troops in Europe?" The shrewd Chou En-lai saw the point, smiled warmly, and changed the subject.

Also cool to the idea of a European security conference was Washington, aided by the more pro-American of the European allies. For Russia had begun by suggesting that the US should be excluded from this strictly European gathering. That would have meant a complete reorientation of Europe toward Moscow, and it seems likely that the Russians made so radical a proposal only in order to create a big bargaining point on which a concession could quickly be made.

But even when American participation in the conference was assured, there remained the uneasy fear that the meeting might lead to some form of pan-European commission which would be a Soviet foot in the door of Western politics. That dread of Russia's gradually gaining an unofficial veto power over the actions of European nations was and is very real.

Nonetheless, Washington couldn't keep objecting to a European security conference when the US itself was actively holding SALT (Strategic Arms Limitation) talks with the Soviets, and the even more controversial MBFR negotiations. The attempt to reach "Mutual and Balanced Force Reductions" was frightening to Europe, because a Russian division moved from East Germany could be back there in fighting condition much faster than an American division that had been flown home. Europe's suspicion that the Americans might be making deals—at the expense of Europe—which would give both the US and Russia things that the two superpowers wanted became a major factor in the Atlantic Alliance. And the more each NATO country gave assurances of its own loyalty to the cause, the more it seemed to be protesting too much.

For practical purposes, then, the Atlantic Alliance became temporarily irrelevant when these bilateral talks were made the rule. It was not destroyed, for no one doubts how fast it would spring to life again if signs of a communist menace became overt and immediate. But every year spent in the limbo of its present low priority has an atrophying effect. And meanwhile the importance of nearby Russia grows in direct proportion to the diminution of the Atlantic relationship. "If Europe continues to make unilateral military concessions to the Soviets and the West becomes provably inferior to the USSR in military capability at the European focal point, then Russia will be a silent participant in every decision we make," Karl Carstens told me early in 1973, shortly before he became floor leader of the Christian Democratic party in Germany's Reichstag. "No government of Europe will consider any important issue without asking itself, 'How will the Soviets like this? What might they do in response to it?' " Conservative European leaders who are trying to prevent the veer away from the Atlantic Alliance privately call this the "Finlandization of Europe." They don't like to sound critical of Finland, whose plight they understand, but they are horrified at the thought of falling into that same abject position. Rather than be forever wondering what would please the Kremlin, as Helsinki must do, they would far rather go back to having Washington as their unseen partner in government.

Men like Carstens unhesitatingly insist that Europeans should pronounce publicly: "You, the Americans, are our firm and *indispensable* allies." They would want the US, in return, to say very loudly: "We are in West Europe to stay. We are there not just to help Europeans, but in order to protect America's enduring vital interests. Nothing can change this." By rekindling such a feeling of identity, they believe, we could obliterate the petty problems that divide us and we could serve the cause of peace by letting the Soviets know just where the line is drawn.

Remembering how many wars America has "started" by not making its resolve clear until an aggressor has been misled into rashness, this kind of approach has an appealing sound. But it is not in sight. A post-Vietnam isolationism on both sides of the Atlantic makes it politically unrealistic. The occasional revival of talk about a "new Atlantic Charter" or a "reaffirmation of our mutual dependence" has no ring of sincerity. If the Duke of Wellington were trying to make the West into a credible alliance today, he would say, as he did before Waterloo, "I have got an infamous army." In the end, he would probably win again; but with the same narrow margin and terrible cost that always come of being an ill-prepared coalition trying to cope with a single great power.

12

Could East Europe Join the EEC?

Up to now it must have seemed as if Russia has things all its own way when it works to soften the West. But think as a Russian again for a few moments, and some very frustrating, even frightening, contradictions will appear.

Russia labors under the terrible handicap of being herself an "underdeveloped country." Imagine trying to maintain a position of international leadership when the world knows that you are vastly inferior to the other superpower in giving your own people the kind of lives they would like. Even more embarrassing, some of the nations you insist on leading are themselves considerably more advanced than your own. That dilemma, in part, was what must have made the Russians shrink in horror from being included in the Marshall Plan. For the US did originally invite Eastern Europe to take part, and some of the satellite nation leaders were set to go along. Suddenly, Moscow made it plain that there would be no such acceptance of capitalist aid.

In the early 1960's Russia faced the problem more concretely when East German workers were being attracted in droves to work in the West. The Berlin Wall, hideous as it is, came only as a desperation move after the roaring boom in West German industry began sucking workers across by the tens of thousands every day. East Germany would soon have been stripped bare of its prime work force.

But the clearest example of Russia's nightmare came in the late 1960's. By that time the Soviets were already anxious to press for more than mere coexistence. They wanted to promote active trade with the West. The most advanced country of the East European bloc, Czechoslovakia, was again producing manufactured goods that met Western standards, as it had done in the old days. But it needed much more in the way of new technology and equipment in order to use the potential of its skilled work force. The West Germans saw a great trade opportunity, and they offered large credits to Czechoslovakia; they would sell the industrial machinery needed, then take some of the finished products for sale in the West. The Czechs, under Alexander Dubček, saw a whole new life opening up to them. Unfortunately, the Czech campus intellectuals were more idealistic than practical. They pressed Dubček to move toward complete political and press freedom at the same time, and he was swept along on the tide. Personally pro-Russian, Dubček found himself in the ludicrous situation of assuring the Soviets that his *free* press would not write anything too objectionable and his *free* elections would not topple the communist regime. Russia might have put up even with the fear that such infectious ideas could spread to other satellites or to the USSR itself; after all, the Kremlin had stood for much worse indignities from Rumania's rebellious government. What really made the situation impossible from Moscow's viewpoint was the spreading arrangement between Czechoslovakia and Germany. For even though the Soviet Union itself planned to move toward closer ties with the Germans, it could not grant that same privilege to an outlying satellite that might be pried away from the Eastern bloc.

"Look at the map, and you'll see at once why Russia must and will send troops into Czechoslovakia," a shrewd analyst in the State Department's European Division told me. The US at that time was publicly voicing confidence that Russia would not move troops against its own satellite. Some of our highest officials apparently believed that, although I know it as a fact that the late Llewellyn Thompson, then our ambassador in Moscow, had concluded that Russia would move in. Only the timing was in doubt. Many of the professionals who saw the picture objectively not only expected the Russian move, but even understood Moscow's dilemma. "The shape of West Germany is like a dagger pointing into East Europe while Czechoslovakia stretches far into the West," one of my informants explained. "If industrial and trade relations are allowed to reach such a point and Dubček's free press keeps speaking out, the moment could easily come when Dubček would suddenly declare Czechoslovakia's withdrawal from the Soviet bloc. Just like these other pronouncements of his, he would assure Russia of the greatest friendship, but just politely declare Czechoslovakia a neutral, somewhat like Austria. Neither side is really ready for such a shake-up in the power balance. Russia would find it ten times as hard to control Prague after such a declaration; and NATO would be pretty embarrassed too by having to decide whether to defend the Czechs or sit on its hands in case of a conflict. So it will be much easier for Brezhnev to move in any day now, before West Germany or the West really has a stake there."

Of course that is just what the Soviets did, and they were able to get most of the other satellites to send in troops also, since each of their governments felt threatened by the revolutionary feelings that Dubček had created. But it was a traumatic decision for Brezhnev, because there was a setback of many months' duration in the USSR's drive to appear friendly, harmless, and freedom-loving to the West. The youth of West Europe, especially, was jarred away from its leftward orientation for a time. But the whole exercise was an object lesson in decisiveness, if one looks at it cynically. "Instead of the bit-by-bit fumbling that most governments, including Russia's, have been practicing in these confusing times, the Kremlin on this occasion saw that there was only one way out, bit the bullet, and did it all as rapidly as possible," an American general told me with professional sang-froid. He was impressed by Russian dexterity in rotating the troops in Prague so that no one unit would have its patience worn down by the angry populace. In that way, exceptional restraint was shown, casualties were very few, and after a new Soviet-backed government had calmed the surface waters for a few months, the people of West Europe had only fuzzy memories of the whole thing. Few know that the former Czech Premier has become—according to one report—director of a motor pool in the city of Bratislava.

But Czechoslovakia—much more than the bloody Hungarian rebellion—must be a live memory in the minds of Soviet policymakers. For an outright revolt crushed by tanks and mortars is a straightforward affair. A move to trade with Germany—when trade with Germany is just what your own government has been preaching—is a much subtler menace.

The European Economic Community, in particular, has become the force that Russia must contend with more than NATO. There are those in both camps who even consider NATO obsolete, because war—the conventional sort that NATO might have some role in—is not the issue in Europe. Under present circumstances, Russia is not even remotely likely to initiate a military confrontation with West Europe. What would be the point? Why have a horde of angry subject people when you can just worry them into acquiescence by your very size and wheedle them into profitable dealings? So a military organization like NATO could be called irrelevant. I don't myself believe that, because I think the thief who walks peacefully past a locked house might well be tempted by an open window; so I would call NATO irrelevant only as long as it exists—*an indispensable relic.*

But even those who hold this view would have to agree that the EEC now is much more to the point in East-West relations. We have already seen that the Common Market is like a huge magnet, attracting to itself every commercial venture that comes anywhere near its field of force. This is true not only in the Free World, but in East Europe as well. From the Community's birth in 1957, its trade with the Soviet bloc grew from 1.8 billion dollars to over nine billion dollars today. Common Market imports from Eastern Europe have been going up twice as fast as imports from other countries; so have the EEC's exports to the East. (Such percentage statistics can be misleading, of course, because they start from a lower base; but the principle they illustrate is very real.)

The Soviet bloc has a "common market" of its own, called the Council for Mutual Economic Assistance, or COMECON. And this has had at least two huge internal problems: one is satellite resentment of Russia's insistence on being the producer of finished products for the group, while the others do the less profitable job of providing raw materials and components. The other is the desire of all COMECON nations to have closer trade and investment ties with the West—the very thing that caused all the trouble in Czechoslovakia. Gradually, Russia's paradoxical situation has forced her to permit more and more of these exchanges. It is not the same kind of trade that the EEC has with the West. East Europe exports mainly primary goods to the Common Market—foods, wood, oil, and coal. And what COMECON buys from the EEC is mostly heavy equipment for use in making its own consumer products. But the figures now amount to very substantial business. Trade between the two Germanies is especially steady and important.

Now further moves are under way to formalize the ties between East and West. Poland and Rumania have joined Czechoslovakia as members of GATT, which has long been a key part of the *Free* World's economic system. Hungary and Bulgaria have also been moving closer to it. These may be steps in the direction of loose ties with the EEC itself. After all, Rumania—always the maverick of the Soviet bloc—asked as early as 1972 to be included in the Common Market's system of generalized trade preferences. This is a long way from membership, but it is an even longer way from the other extreme of economic isolation. And Soviet Party leader Leonid Brezhnev told a Congress of Soviet Labor Unions that the European Community must be recognized as "a fact of life."

This has been more than matched by the EEC's receptive attitude. For now any trade negotiations with East European countries are no longer conducted by individual member states. The Community as a whole deals with the Soviet bloc. Bilateral agreements are not even allowed.

And the communist group will draw nearer to the EEC year by year. Not all of this will be on a bloc basis, regardless of what the rule makers in Brussels dictate. The greatest tie is between the many persons of German origin on the two sides of the old iron curtain. Hardly a family in West Germany is without kin in East Germany. And many are related to persons of German ancestry who live in Czechoslovakia. These family and racial ties promote letter writing, telephoning, and visits across borders.

The tourist industry itself is now a major link between East and West. Any airport in Europe has an assortment of Russian, Polish, and Hungarian airliners being refueled or boarded. Most major cities see busloads of tourists from Leipzig, Prague, or Budapest leaning out to snap pictures, looking much like any other tourist group. This kind of travel does not—as was observed in an earlier chapter—make for firm political links between nations; but it tears big gaps in the Soviet-led attempt to isolate the bloc from the infection of Western pay scales, Western goods, and Western information.

The exchange of specialized technical equipment also brings about a meshing of peoples. England or France cannot simply pack a complex new automated production line in so many crates and ship them to Bucharest. First the Rumanians send teams of their specialists to watch such a system operating in Nottingham or Lyons. Then the selling company sends some of its top men to Rumania, perhaps for months, to set things in place and watch the early operations.

More important even than this is the fact that the East Europeans look to the West as one of their main markets. When their new industries are producing well, they expect to sell a part of their production to the countries that sold them the equipment. Some of the deals, in fact, stipulate such a trade-off as payment for the equipment. And since East Europe's labor still is very low-wage compared to the West, these products will be very serious competition for European and American industries.

So it is highly probable that a steady intertwining of East and West European business affairs will develop. And this will be paralleled by treaties and working arrangements that go well beyond anything now in existence.

The larger question of whether any East European nation can one day actually join the EEC and take part in the Brussels policymaking is quite another matter. That would require a real revolution—not so much in the East as in the West. It would mean that the European Community had given up all its Atlantic orientation, all its links with an American-led NATO. This is most unlikely, as poor as US-European relations are. For, as noted before, Europe's ultimate dependence for its peace and freedom is on the USA. We can assume that it will not voluntarily exchange dependence on Washington for subjection to Moscow.

13

Europe's Long Reach

The Mediterranean, the Middle East, Africa, the Caribbean, the Pacific: into all these areas the hand of Brussels has stretched. It goes well beyond the periphery of Europe—almost to the whole world.

But it would be misleading to see all of this as part of one Community policy to capture vast new territories. Nor is it seen that way in Washington. For, strangely enough, the US policymakers are less disturbed by accords made in "our own" Caribbean than by agreements with Sweden or Spain.

The European Community is not really reaching—as a unified Community—for much that is new. Its individual members are making sure they don't give up what they had before. Each EEC country that formerly was a colonial power or that had close commercial links with some less-developed nation is now trying to retain that lucrative old tie, while enjoying the new fruits of membership in a bigger group. Each one makes its old colonial relationships the basis of its new policy toward Africa and Asia. When it comes to technical assistance, for example, here is where the Common Market countries place their priorities:

- Belgium gives most to Zaire, the former Belgian Congo.
- France makes Algeria its No. 1 recipient.
- Germany, long separated from colonial holdings, gives

most to India, which is a principal customer for German plants and machinery.

· Italy gives most to Somalia, Libya, and Ethiopia, all areas where it had past interests.

· The Netherlands sends technical aid mainly to Indonesia.

· England aids Kenya most, followed by Zambia and other former British colonies.

In much the same way, as we have seen earlier, the EEC gives special tariff preferences to these and other poorer countries, allowing crops from African states to come in at better rates than those from, say, Latin America. But as many of these crops were raised on French-owned or British-owned farms, the colonial investors of France, Britain, Belgium, and the rest are really exchanging favors with each other. The former preferential treatment in a single nation is now exchanged for the great plum of Community-wide access. Much of this doesn't distress Washington, because it only reinforces old relationships and preferences that the US never objected to before.

In a minor way it does affect some of our own client states. If a certain African crop that formerly had special access only to France now gets similar favors in Italy, Germany, Denmark, and so on, some Latin-American sales to Europe could be displaced. The Latins used to look mainly to the US for help in getting a square deal from Europe. When Costa Rica, Honduras, or Jamaica, for example, feared that the former French colonies in Africa would take over their banana markets in Europe, they first asked Washington to press Brussels for assurances that this would not happen. Gradually, though, they found that they could speak for themselves just as effectively. In fact, European countries with a growing interest in finding investment opportunities in Latin America might be a little more attentive to intense pleas directly from the Latins than they were to mild pressures from Americans who had other things on their minds. So now ministers from twenty-two Latin-American republics often go to Brussels as a group to meet with the Commission. Whether it is the persuasiveness of this diplomacy or—as some insist—simply a matter of quality and price, the fact is that Latin America's banana exports to the EEC have not slipped at all. Nor has trade in most of the other commodities that are so important to the southern half of this hemisphere.

Most Latin-American countries now have diplomatic relations with the EEC, just as though it were a nation. Some of them appoint two or three additional men in their regular embassy to Belgium to handle EEC matters.

If the Latins do still look to the US for help along these lines, it is mainly to solicit cash aid whenever their overseas trade in a certain commodity has deteriorated—usually due to world market conditions, rather than EEC devices. Washington still privately relishes the vestiges of Latin America's dependence and wishes there were more of it. So any vexation it feels has little to do with European unfairness to the Latin republics. What irks the US, rather, is Europe's tendency to aggrandize its stake both in this hemisphere and in Africa, and then to press America to participate in schemes that would build up European income from its own ex-colonies.

Here is a broad picture of the EEC's agreements with territories beyond Europe—and bear in mind that some of these are simply trade agreements, others are "association agreements," which usually include economic and technical aid and co-operation:

· There is a group of Mediterranean accords. In addition to Greece and Spain, already mentioned in the previous chapter, these are with Turkey, Israel, Malta, Morocco, Portugal, Tunisia, Yugoslavia, Cyprus, Egypt, and Lebanon. Interest in similar arrangements has been expressed by Algeria, Jordan, and Syria. (Notice one of the advantages of a loose organization that can deny its nationhood whenever convenient: no single country could have a close tie with Israel and with several rabidly anti-Zionist Arab states at the same time. The EEC has done so for years, because it could "blame" different ones of its member nations for each half of the policy.)

· Some thirty African nations, mostly the former colonies of EEC member states, are now associate members. The right to link up in this way has also been offered to a few that had no strict colonial ties with EEC nations: Ethiopia, Liberia, and Equatorial Guinea, which was once Spanish.

· And another dozen potential associates in the Caribbean and the Indian and Pacific Oceans are being spoken of. For example, former Commonwealth countries in the Caribbean may form a small local bloc of their own, then associate the entire group with the EEC.

What are these deals like? What does it mean to be an associate member? Take the relatively recent agreement with Lebanon as one example. It was concluded because of France's interest in that country. It grants special tariff cuts of forty-five per cent to well over half of Lebanese industrial exports to the Community, and it gives some concessions on a major group of Lebanese farm products. In return, Lebanon grants customs reductions on a wide range of imports from the Community. The eventual goal is to achieve a "free-trade area" between Lebanon and the Community. The deal with Egypt is much the same. And an arrangement made with Cyprus—which has since been jeopardized in the 1974 fighting there—goes further and makes Cyprus an associate of the EEC, with the stated intent of negotiating an almost complete removal of all trade barriers (but not full membership) by the late 1970's.

The past effects of such deals on trade have been substantial, although sometimes below expectations. Exports from the associates to the EEC have grown by an average of six to seven per cent yearly, but this is no more than the growth of all developing country sales to the Community. And the EEC's sales in return have also been roughly the same as their sales to poorer nations in general. The figures are not very meaningful because the instability of raw-materials prices produced by such countries makes the year-to-year variation very large. In many cases, it is not trade preference, but some kind of price stabilizing fund that is wanted most. In simpler words, aid. The Community buys about two-thirds of the exports of the associate nations and sells them about two-thirds of their imports. But free trade is not as magical a word to such countries as it is in the affluent world. Simply a decline in the world market price of cocoa, for example, can mean years of depression for Ghana. What such nations want is outright economic aid, plus price-propping schemes whereby the developed countries assure them that the raw materials sold will earn enough to pay for the ever-rising cost of the machinery and equipment that must be imported. They also want a great deal of technical help in developing new uses for tropical products and new ways of processing them. All this costs money. And it helps to explain why the US is inclined to let Europe continue to be the No. 1 friend of the "Third World." Since it is European companies and investors that will benefit most in the end, let Europe's taxpayers be the ones to send development aid now.

The US has raised objections to any hint of reverse preferences granted by the developing nations to Europe.

In other words, we don't want Europe to use its leverage to force an African country to grant tariff reductions only to the EEC nations. The latter hastily say that they would not think of imposing on the sovereignty of a poorer state. "We are working toward a free-trade area," the Europeans insist, "with reduction of all tariffs to zero between ourselves and the associate countries. We will not tell the associate what it must do; if it wishes to grant the same zero-duty favor to the US and others, that is its affair." Washington remains skeptical and firmly opposed to reverse preferences. But knowing that they are bound to exist, it is hard to escape the impression that this is just a bargaining card that the US likes to show occasionally.

In working out their new set of relationships with the developing countries, Europe and America can at least feel relief on one point: it is finally being recognized that agriculture may be much more important than industry for many nations. During most of the fizzy years of high development after World War II everything combined to give poorer countries the impression that only industrialization could make them well off. A few prophetic voices tried to say otherwise. Harvard's Gottfried Haberler, for example, was one of the first to remind that a country like New Zealand had achieved a very high living standard by heavy concentration on good agricultural production, while the rapid building of clusters of factories might lead only to uncompetitive industries, disillusioned workers grouped in squalid cities, and an actual loss in the nation's power to create human contentment. But it took courage and a taste for frustration to say such things to the heads of developing nations in those days. They were likely to assume that the representative of a wealthy country was just trying to preserve the status quo in his own favor.

And then for many years it was hard to answer the argument that raw-materials prices tend to move up much more slowly than manufactured-goods prices. So the man or nation that produced from the land was usually at a disadvantage in exchanging his wares with those of a factory. Now there is some change in this, as waves of commodity shortages sometimes seem to make the products of the land most desirable of all. But the arithmetic has been slow to bear it out. When in 1973 wheat or wool hit figures that the newspapers described as "historic highs," they had taken over a century to do what manufactured goods had been doing year after year. Now it appears that food prices may stay on a higher trend and take up a larger part of each person's spending power. Even so, the sharp sudden changes in price—the dips when there is a bumper crop and the soaring values in time of drought—are inescapable. Some less-developed nations may often find themselves with a good crop of one main product, yet woefully short of rice or wheat for subsistence.

So food will be a principal determinant of power in the world. It is one of America's mightiest weapons, for our geography enables us to produce a greater variety and quantity of foodstuffs and feed grains than any other area. But Europe is and will remain very much in the contest of using food production as a way to extend national influence.

The urge to be cynical about every decision of an institution that is, after all, dealing with cynical subjects should not prevent us from acknowledging that the EEC's grasp for more power in the world is not the sole explanation of its substantial food-aid programs. There was a time when it seemed that America was a nonpareil—the only country that consistently gave and gave whenever there was disaster or famine somewhere in the world. Now it should be known that our European forebears, being of the same essence as ourselves, have the same tendency when their means begin to approach our own.

Recently, for example, the EEC sent very large amounts of food to displaced persons in Cambodia, Laos, North Vietnam, and South Vietnam—such things as husked rice, powdered milk, and sugar. And within days of that, the EEC Commission approved a large allocation to save the lives of people caught in one of the worst African droughts in years—in Chad, Mali, Mauritania, Niger, Senegal, the Republic of Upper Volta and many other nations.

These emergency shipments are in addition to nearly a half-million tons of cereal grains annually that is sent to developing nations under an agreement dating back several years. If Europe's share is only a little more than half the amount pledged by the US, bear in mind that the relative production of such foods and the relative living standards of the two continents make Europe's contribution a greater sacrifice than our own. The Community also sends substantial amounts of dairy products to the poorer nations. The total amount of food aid given by the Community now reaches over one hundred million dollars per year, and this is over and above the much larger aid granted to the African countries that are associated with the EEC.

If it is hoped that food to Indochina or Bangladesh will someday earn Europe a better image or a little more privilege in those areas, that need not make us see the whole exercise as strictly business. Aid very often develops business ties. The US foreign-aid program was a prime example of that, and yet we know that business was not the chief aim. It is pleasanter and more objective to see it as a happy side effect.

But the sum total of the EEC's relations with the less-developed world does have to be seen as an example of

Europe's growing rivalry with the US. In almost every area where England once was great or France or Belgium once was great, the EEC group now is—if not exactly great—distinctly important. It should have big implications for our political as well as our commercial policies. The US need not wish to be the world's sole great power. But in that case, it should not be expected to bear quite so much of the policeman's responsibility either. Why should the EEC have a business role anywhere near as large as our own in Indochina or the Indian Ocean or the Mediterranean, and yet have a much smaller share in the defense of those areas? It is not so much the *length* of Europe's reach as the inexpensiveness of it that will increasingly concern Washington policymakers. In looking for ways to balance up the distorted accounts between America and Europe, a rearrangement of the defense postures could play a big part.

14

Energy: The Surprises Ahead

It is commonly believed that the energy crisis of 1973–74 caused cracks both in Europe and in the Atlantic Community, and turned the West from high prosperity to a grim fight against looming disaster.

I question this. The prosperity had been fragile for years before that. The cracks were already there. Fuel problems only illuminated the truth.

There is a vast difference between true scarcity and inability to meet abnormal demand. If the world's use of newsprint, for example, grew to a point where producers could dictate any terms at all, it should not be called a paper shortage, but an excess of publishing. If tremendous farm production failed to keep pace with escalating demands for more food per capita, it would deserve the name of gluttony rather than famine. Such things would indicate something so wrong in the way people were living that they would be bound to create one kind or another of critical problem. Deprivation, in that case, might be the least of the evils.

So it is with energy. Since the overuse of fuel was poisoning the world, is it reasonable to bemoan limitation of the supply? The 1973 oil embargo following the Arab-

Israeli confrontation was possible only because the West's way of living had invited it. The unnatural pace of industrial growth would soon have worked even greater havoc on man if providence had not taken a hand.

Energy had been misused ever since the end of World War II. Cheap fuel, especially from the Mideast, had been abused to make the modern nations abnormally active. I do not use the word "rich," because that is a dangerous euphemism to describe the frenzy and soot that the industrial growth of the 1950's and 1960's had created. The Arab refusal to go on stepping up production should have been viewed as a bitter but salutary antidote. Their sharp price increases—although belated, too harsh, and much too sudden—were another move in the same direction, and potentially beneficial. For prohibitive cost can be almost as effective a check on abuse as outright lack of supplies.

So the real life-and-death issue for the Atlantic Community is not whether enough energy can be dredged up, but whether the opportunity to take a healthy new turn will be seized. Will national leaders use this sudden enforced halt of pernicious growth as a moment for also checking inflation? Will they prove the viability of the EEC and the Atlantic Community by showing that these groups can co-operate when a really difficult issue arises? Up to now, the signs are not good. There was an EEC contingency plan for joint action in fuel crises, and there was also a NATO plan; neither one was given much heed when the Arab squeeze came. But if the modern countries continue to work at cross-purposes, it will not mean a victory for their adversaries. The surprise in store for Arabs and communists is that they may suffer most of all.

Men who are most foresighted in their awareness of American-European interdependence have urged much greater co-operation. "It should be unthinkable, after so many great achievements," says Egidio Ortona, Italy's ambassador to Washington, "that the two continents—and, in fact, all the nations that produce or consume oil—should not co-operate closely in their policies and assure a steady supply at fair prices."

The energy history of the twentieth century shows why such pleas are overridden. Energy is life. In poorer nations that live simply, man's own energy determines at what level life will be lived. In our part of the world what passes for contentment has depended on the rapid movement of wheels and turbines and electrons, and this kind of "life" has been produced mainly by burning oil or gas. The escalating demand for these fuels has far outpaced the ability of exploring oil countries to develop new sources. They have made great finds—in Alaska, Indonesia, the North Sea, and even off the coast of China. But all of these combined have not been enough to keep fuel oil, gasoline, and natural gas from becoming scarcer and more expensive.

One area alone has made all the difference: the Middle East. It has been said that oil there is so plentiful, so near the surface, that just stamping on the ground will cause a gusher to spring up next to the footprint. Until very recently a few oil companies from the West were able to buy this liquid gold very cheaply and with apparently no end in sight. Their payments for the concessions were more than enough to make the few ruling sheiks and emirs extremely rich, so anyone who had anything to say on the subject was entirely satisfied. Then came a series of changes in the structure of several Middle Eastern countries. Zionists carved a dedicated nation from land that Palestinians felt was their own. Egypt's monarch was deposed, and Nasser made anti-Zionism into a pan-Arab crusade. The King of Iraq was assassinated, and a leftist regime took over.

The Arab-Israeli Six-Day War in 1967 was second only

to the Vietnam War as a disaster for American foreign policy. The losing side, resentful of Washington's anti-Arab position, was the one with the oil. Among the modern countries, only two emerged as victors: the Soviet Union and France. Both had decided, as a cold-blooded matter of national policy, to stand as friends of the Arabs. That led to a situation in which the Soviet Union began to acquire growing amounts of Mideast oil, some of which it passes on to Western Europe in order to build up dependence on herself as a source of supply. France stands well with the Algerian oil suppliers, their former colonials, as well as with most other Arab states. Japan, by moving in quickly and offering very liberal terms, got access to large oil supplies. But the US and many of the countries of Europe found themselves constantly embroiled in commercial disputes and often on the brink of broken relations.

The next major blow came when a zealous military junta replaced the ruler of Libya. It proved to be the most aggressive of all in taking over ownership of foreign oil interests and keeping more of the profits. As one new Mideast regime after another began to demand far more money from the oil "exploiters" in order to benefit their own countries, the remaining older rulers were pushed in the same direction. For one thing, the idea of larger revenues was appealing. And for another, they had to give their own people the feeling that a monarchy looks out for its citizens as well as a republic does.

After the second Arab-Israeli war, the oil embargo declared by King Faisal of Saudi Arabia late in 1973 signaled still another turn: a monarchist counterattack against republicanism in the Arab world. Note that well, for it was much more the issue than the Arab crusade that served as a convenient screen. The monarchs, anxious as they are to help the Palestinians and to retake Jerusalem from the Jews, cannot really have the same goals as the Arab colonels and presidents who have tried to knock them off their very thrones. Nor can they share in the willingness to have Soviet Russia as a principal ally. King Faisal and his fellow monarchs were mainly out to strengthen their own positions. The non-Arab Shah of Iran, who opposed the embargo but led the drive to increase oil *prices,* had the equally reasonable aim of making his petroleum comparable to other forms of energy in the world scale of values. The energy in Mideast oil had been priced at a small fraction of the equivalent energy in coal and other fuels, he argued. Why should any nation be willing to sell off a nonrenewable asset at bargain rates?

Up, up, and up went the price that these nations charged for oil and the share of participation in the total revenue that they demanded. The oil companies of the West, while bemoaning the good old days, still found the arrangement profitable. Higher costs of production were eventually passed along to the users back home. But each nation of Europe, North America, and Japan found that its total bill for oil from the Mideast was rising alarmingly. Suddenly this became the greatest commercial revolution in the history of man. A few very underdeveloped nations with a relatively small total population of extremely backward people had become a major business force with ability to dictate terms to the rest of the world.

But look ahead now to the continuing facts that will outlive the adjustment period of the mid 1970's:

· The oil-producing nations will not be as unified as they have been able to appear in the first few years of the decade. Intense concentration on fighting a common enemy focused the Arab mind and will; but that intensity will be dissipated by piecemeal settlement of issues.

· Neither will these nations retain the initial level of determination to have all their own way with the consuming countries. Once the oilmen of the West had scoffed at the idea of the Arabs cutting off supplies. "They need us as customers more than we need them," was one common attitude. And the conviction that "they can't drink the oil" gave America and Europe undue confidence for years. But although these Westerners proved to be too sanguine, there is still validity in this view—and perhaps more in the future than there was before. *One of the great Arab strengths came from their low living standard.* They didn't *need* trade with the West in order to survive. Unlike us, they were not so dependent on things imported from the outside world. The less they needed in the way of consumer imports and machinery, the better they could outlast the West in a confrontation. But now this ascetic durability will be subverted by the growing emphasis on development. Like everyone else, the Arabs will be weakened by success.

· The Arabs will lose their strong position in UN politics and other relations with the developing nations if they continue a fuel-price policy that would bankrupt these less-developed countries. While such an intangible factor may not weigh as heavily as cold cash, it has a very practical effect on how vulnerable the oil producers might be to the use of force by great powers. Would any Mideast country want to feel, for instance, that an invasion of its oil fields by desperate European powers on a fabricated charge would meet with smiles and nods of approval from scores of poorer countries?

· The Kremlin cannot permanently support too extreme a policy on oil prices. For world leadership purposes, Moscow cares about the good opinion of the poor nations, too, and would jeopardize that if it failed to pressure its Arab friends to moderate their ways. Besides, the Soviets cannot relish the higher price their aid to the Arabs costs, now that Russian barter agreements with the Mideast have to conform to the price scales met by European nations.

· Even if they decided to resist all these pressures, the oil-producing countries would have to face the fact that they could reap only a few years of such huge oil revenues. The higher the price of Mideast fuel, the more practical becomes every other scheme for developing alternate sources. Drilling in offshore or distant areas that might have been neglected before gets a new priority from American, European, and Japanese planners. So does extraction of oil from sands in the US and Canada. The economics of nuclear power suddenly seems much brighter. Even costly projects for using solar energy are advanced from the year 2000 to the 1980's.

· Discoveries of oil and gas in the North Sea will give Britain a fuel *surplus* before this decade ends. With energy to spare, London will not want to depress fuel prices unduly, but it can help Europe to escape Arab domination.

All these reasons, growing in vigor, will force a moderating of the Arab position. No price cutback to the level of the early 1970's is foreseeable, unless a serious economic downturn cuts demand severely. But over the next several years oil prices *relative to other goods* will average less than the trend seen in 1974 might lead one to suppose.

Did the bright young English-trained economists who counsel Arab sheiks and colonels fail to do their homework thoroughly when they allowed the pace of price increases to risk all these changes in the minds of their customers? Didn't they advise their employers to step up the rates gradually enough to avoid such a reaction? Almost certainly they did give wiser counsel. The abrupt shift to a reckless path probably proves that even at that moment of apparent unity the oil producers were split. And when the Saudi

Arabian embargo and the fear of shortages made the West panic and grasp for supplies, no Mideast government could refrain from scrambling to get its share of the booty. It is the same attitude that would—and perhaps will—cause them to cut prices competitively if demand should one day slacken.

In the meanwhile, however, the shift of money from industrial nations to those of the Mideast makes fantastic changes in both camps. Saudi Arabia's revenues could reach more than fifty billion dollars annually within a few years. Kuwait may have fifteen billion dollars in yearly revenues by the end of this decade. And a similar income is possible for even smaller Abu Dhabi. The states of the Arabian peninsula alone—not to mention other major producers such as Iran and Iraq—may have total monetary reserves in the neighborhood of 250 billion dollars by 1980.

This is potentially enough to make every citizen of the Arab world rich and cared for to the point of indolence. It is a grave question for each of these countries to decide whether to invest the money in the outside world for long-term benefits, or to construct harbors, roads, and other foundations for future modernization, or to move at once toward raising living standards with welfare policies, hospitals, schools, and so on. Some, like King Faisal of Saudi Arabia, are commonly believed to be secretly in favor of dragging their feet on education and industrialization. And this is not necessarily because they are selfish men who care only for their own wealth. Some of them genuinely believe that their people today are better off than they will be when they emulate countries with big industrial populations that cluster in unnatural metropolitan centers.

But the problems within the Arab world—problems of fantastic sudden prosperity—concern us here only to the extent that they will create changes in America and Europe.

The Atlantic Community countries will have a trade deficit of hundreds of billions of dollars yearly in dealings with their oil suppliers. There is not enough cash to pay for this, so we must give the oil-producing countries a share in our economy. Some of this is salutary. The process began when the Shah of Iran bid for a half-interest in a chain of US gasoline stations in return for a promise to deliver certain amounts of oil over a long period of years. A ruler is much less likely to cut off petroleum supplies if that would result in closing down his own gas pumps in America. Other oil-producing countries are arranging similar and much larger deals to acquire refineries and gasoline-distributing facilities in the US. But the amounts of money owed to the Mideast will be so huge that even these agreements will fall far short of balancing the books. Much bigger transfers will be required. We and Europe must, in effect, hand over vast amounts of our assets to the Arabs. It will be said that they are "investing" in our economies. But cutting through the intermediate steps, it really means that they will be taking shares of steel and computer and aircraft companies in return for barrels of oil.

The trend toward betterment for the Mideast nations would be laudable, if it were not for the abruptness of it. The sense of revolution, rather than well-earned evolution, makes it objectionable, even from the viewpoint of some Arabs. And from the American and European standpoint, it is not easy to think of these as normal investments when they are coupled with coercion. Like a player in a Monopoly game who lacks ready money, we are being forced to sell off some prize holdings.

But apart from business assets, America does have many bargaining weapons in the fight for oil and gas. US military might is, in itself, precious to Mideast nations as a balancing force that prevents Russia from dominating them. Some of the most advanced technology can still be obtained only from the United States. And one of our main trading chips is the other great energy fuel that was discussed in the last chapter: food. "When people say we're short of gold to pay for oil and other things we need, I tell them food is our gold," US Agriculture Secretary Earl Butz once said. "We can produce more food, more cheaply and more efficiently, than any other part of the world." Butz had to soften that boast in late 1974, for the need to hold down prices at home made the US reluctant to expand food *aid*. But commercial food exports will remain high. This advantage is almost certain to stay with us, for it derives not only from technology, but also from climate. Most of Russia is farther north than the US-Canadian border. As her living standards rise, and the people want upgraded food supplies, such as meat, Russia's need for feed grains as well as wheat will oftener than not outstrip her production of these things. America can help to supply them, and can demand in return a certain amount of Russian co-operation in selling us liquefied natural gas directly or in moving Mideast oil to us indirectly.

But the greatest of all American weapons is sheer size and buying power. Being a huge market, the biggest customer in the world, gives an irreplaceable importance. Suppliers tend to forget this in times when their goods are in great demand. But if they push too far and spoil that customer's prosperity, what have they left then?

We are just now seeing a surge of confidence on the part of nations that supply all sorts of raw materials to the industrialized world. Finding their goods in great demand, the countries that produce commodities now feel that they can copy the example of the fuel-producing nations and take over the driver's seat. But they are under the illusion that raw materials or energy are things of great value in themselves. That is not so. Their value depends entirely on the desire and ability of modern countries to convert them into consumer goods or comforts. If the great nations are pushed into depression, fuel and raw materials will suddenly become drugs on the world market. The misery of the backward nations will be worse than ever before. That is the surprise in store for the Atlantic Community and its suppliers in the years to come—the fact that *the power to dictate supply and price policies will revert to the modern world and especially to the USA.*

This introduces a very complicated by-play between the US and Europe. If American food and American joint ventures with the Arab countries bring fuel to the US, will America also use its bargaining leverage to assure that the Mideast supplies fuels to West Europe as well? Yes—if. If the Europeans are co-operative in accepting the monetary and trade arrangements that Washington urges. Otherwise, Europe will have to shift for itself in its search for fuel. But that search might lead along paths that would be most distressing to Washington. It could mean more West European reliance on Russian fuel—already somewhat alarmingly begun by piped natural gas from the Soviet Union into southern Europe. A Europe that relies too heavily on Russia for fuel could no longer be an ally or military buffer against that supplier.

Apart from price or quantities, Europe might also rush to get ahead of America in meeting still another Arab ambition. Several of the Middle Eastern countries argue that it is their duty to exchange their declining and unrenewable natural resource only in return for something as permanent as industrialization. And so they invite large companies of America, Japan, or Europe to come and establish in the Mideast industries that require huge amounts of energy—such as processing bauxite into aluminum or making iron ore into steel. This is a departure from all normal industrial behavior, for it means carrying the raw materials to a distant place and then shipping the finished products to other faraway markets. But the Arabs have fantastic amounts of energy that is going to waste, such as the ten million or more cubic feet of natural gas that is flared away each day. They also have large numbers of low-cost laborers. And most of all they have the power to reward the co-operative nations with oil preferences. Europe and Japan, desperate to increase oil supplies, have hastened to encourage some of their industries to build plants in the Mideast. That will not only play a part in the petroleum flow; it will also confront some major US industries with competition from a new source of low-cost products.

This only provides beginning insights into the struggle that America and Europe are likely to wage over energy. Both continents face the paradox—which may come to be repeated with other essential raw materials—of seeing former colonies and "backward countries" move into important financial positions. By working together, the Atlantic nations could control and stabilize the trade patterns. It would be enlightened self-interest for either side of the ocean to go more than halfway to accommodate the other. Washington, by sharing its fuel leverage with Europe, could revitalize the alliance and gain in its world position. Europe, by abstaining from short-term expediency, could keep itself more secure. If history is any guide, America and Europe will co-operate just enough to get supplies from the commodity-rich countries, but not enough to prevent roller-coaster prices. They will compete among themselves and thus let energy become one more cause of discord within the Atlantic Community.

15

The Environment Rebels

"In the early 1900's there were so many salmon in the Rhine river that housemaids working near its banks grew tired of having fish for dinner so often," Joseph Luns points out. "Some of them got together and stipulated in their work agreements that they were not to be fed salmon more than three times per week. Nowadays, the Rhine is too polluted to support many fish. A news photographer recently dramatized this by developing a picture under its waters. The Rhine made a very acceptable dark room."

In spirit, if not in very tangible form, concern over this problem bridges the Atlantic—and even the Pacific—more than most present-day issues. If the co-operation to do something about it is not very concrete, the talk among nations is voluminous. It was a European who first organized a group of global thinkers to ponder it; then an American study team was appointed to analyze it by computer; and later the whole world was riveted and appalled by the conclusions.

Italian industrialist Aurelio Peccei put together the loosely knit "Club of Rome"—a collection of thinkers from almost all countries—to debate whether the world is about to suffocate or starve itself. Putting it this way makes it clear that shortages of fuel or other commodities do not at all settle the environmentalists' worries. For it is not just pollution, per se, that the Club of Rome and others of like mind are concerned about. It is the habitability of our planet, the adequacy of all life-supporting resources. This group inspired and financed a study by the Massachusetts Institute of Technology which stunned the world with its announcement that man was near the last possible moment for saving his planet and himself from extinction. Unless the present rate of resource consumption is ended within the next few years, the report "Limits of Growth" said, there will be no way to avert a series of appalling disasters within decades which could badly impair or entirely demolish civilization. Yet, as man will do, the nations are still giving little more than lip service to the notion that something had best be done.

For one thing, there is genuine controversy about whether the danger is really all that bad or grossly exaggerated. Tapping new mineral resources on the moon and on other planets has been suggested. More immediately practical, the harnessing of solar energy by means of giant reflectors orbiting the earth could provide easy, cheap, and perfectly clean power for cities and other stationary purposes. And it is said that much of our manufacturing could be done in orbiting stations—getting some of the benefits of zero gravity and a high vacuum, while avoiding pollution of our own planet. The men who make such proposals deny that growth must be curbed.

But the controversy, real as it is, is also a convenient excuse to delay actions that no one wants to face. Far from rushing to resolve the disagreements, governments delight in the fact that they rule out any prompt decision making. Each country's concern is to dodge financial responsibility as much as possible, even for ecological problems that it clearly helps to create or that take place on its doorstep. Holland, for example, has been called "the sewer of

Europe," because all the pollution that flows along the Rhine finally comes to its mouth in the Netherlands. And so the Dutch, who spend more per capita than any other people in the world to fight pollution, ask their neighbors to contribute to the clean-up cost. But the others have usually had a ready answer. "You Dutch get rich on all the activity that pollutes the Rhine," they say. "Look at the huge fees you get on all the river traffic coming through there. Anything you spend on fighting pollution is just a normal business expense."

In Europe, as in the US, the few real actions against the problems of pollution have come mainly from youth groups and radical elements. A man like Roel van Duyn, who describes himself as an anarchist, but who runs a quite well-knit political party, has roused enough people in Holland by means of his books and talks to win a number of seats on the Amsterdam City Council. He especially detests the automobile and the roadways that it requires. "By the end of the century we will have occupied twenty per cent of our surface with highways," he forecasts, calling the automobile a dangerous product that detracts from the availability of good food, air, and water. He would like to see energy derived from wind and solar sources, rather than from petrochemical processes that harm the environment. But even if such views seem extreme, the activism behind them does produce results, some critics have to agree. The head of Holland's Physical Planning Agency admits that the pressure of these extremist groups has finally led to the passage of air and water laws that he had been vainly recommending since 1964.

Once-beautiful areas of Italy are an example of some of the worst problems and the greatest lethargy. The pull of workers away from farms and into the cities is particularly aggravated in the peninsula. About half of Italy's fifty-four million people now live in metropolitan regions along Italy's coasts which make up only eight per cent of the country's area. This has produced a sharp surge in all kinds of city problems, including viral hepatitis. Yet Italy spends less on ecological research than any other member of the EEC. Only a half of one per cent of her gross national income is spent on the environment, as compared with two to three per cent in some other Western nations.

What has the EEC as a group done about this? Not very much that is real up to now. It has issued a few directives that touch on subjects affecting all nations. For example, a strict control on the "biodegradability" of detergents—the rate at which they dissolve into harmlessness—has been set up by the EEC Commission. And late in 1973 the Council of Ministers agreed on *goals* for the first Environment Policy—a two-year program calling for action by the Community as a whole and by individual members. This contained some admirable statements of objectives: To prevent, reduce, and, where possible, eliminate pollution; to maintain a satisfactory ecological balance; to exploit resources without damaging ecological balances; and so on. It also set forth some general principles for how the policy should work, including the point that polluters themselves should pay for antipollution measures. And special mention was made of trying to agree on steps to reduce pollution of the Rhine river. Now it remains to be seen how much meaningful action the countries can really agree on, and how soon they start it. The past history of all companies and communities that are asked to take antipollution measures at their own expense gives cause to suppose that small first steps are the most to expect.

As for the Atlantic Community and the other nations of the world, their co-operation has also been of the sketchiest kind. Knowing this is vital to grasping a key fact that helps to foresee the whole Atlantic future: man's intellect has not grown, nor his sense of long-term responsibility, and the Atlantic countries will do nothing real about their severest problems until disaster impends. NATO has tried to make the ecology one of its concerns—partly in order to buttress its own reasons for existence. And there are sporadic meetings among a few scientific men of the allied nations. In addition, there have been attempts to pretend that all countries, including the communists, are co-operating mightily on this subject. But the first large international meeting held in Sweden to find common approaches quickly degenerated into a propaganda session in which Peking and Moscow tried to outmaneuver each other, and both shot barbs at Washington. The Swedish Prime Minister veered away from the usual courtesies of a conference host and attacked American policy in Indochina as an example of destruction of the environment.

Ill-judged or ill-timed as that complaint was, it does highlight a fact that makes it hard to shake off pessimism about the future of America and Europe if they persist in encouraging each other to be more technologically developed. The greater the advancement along scientific lines, the greater the capacity—and apparently the tendency—to use it destructively. The dropping of thousands of tons of huge bombs on relatively small areas of Indochina—whatever the political goals—simply appears as lunacy if thought of in objective terms. Think what the world's most advanced people—those presumably with the greatest stake in the future—have been doing to their own globe in the years of "peace" since 1945. Apart from the bombs and the nuclear tests, there are the deadlier daily defacings that we come to take for granted: the most beautiful seacoasts or lakes are scarred with high-rise condominiums, rivers are fouled with noxious wastes, buildings that have just been erected or steam-cleaned begin to blacken within weeks, green Europe and spacious America are repaved with millions of acres of asphalt. All these are so clearly deformations of nature that some people see a biblical significance in them. But it takes no specially prophetic turn of mind to know that auto industries grinding out millions of cars yearly and being always exhorted by investors and by politicians to produce more and more of the same are unsustainable. Even if the glut of cars or the inflated cost of fueling them doesn't kill the whole process, the sheer monotony of cities and highways and cloverleaves will lessen the desire to travel. Just in the last few years we have witnessed several forms of human rebellion that overthrew statistically based forecasts—a sharp drop in the desire for children, refusal by some assembly-line workers to tolerate repetitious work beyond a certain point, a conscious turn by many college students away from the most remunerative careers. It will be surprising if average families do not also rebel at the high cost of buying and driving more and more vehicles that can only move along dreary roads between drab terminal points.

It is not the fault of political leaders, who must constantly be jockeying for job tenure, that none of this meets their definition of a crisis. A crisis in the political lexicon is a scandal that threatens the Administration, or a sudden wave of unemployment and rioting, or an enemy power putting missiles within striking range. An economy based on dirt and artificial fibers and artificial food; a society full of boredom, rushing from city to city by car and finding them all alike, then being shot from country to country by plane and finding them more alike too, a people whose children don't want to face growing up and whose adults yearn to be children—this is not considered a crisis.

Well, it is a crisis. Not really because of pollution, for scientists could probably find ways to contain its worst effects; but because of the senselessness, the loss of touch with the natural environment. Just outside Geneva, Switzerland, there is a beautiful lakefront that stretches for many kilometers and a drive that once was idyllic. Now a bigger and bigger road has been built to accommodate the increasing numbers of cars that pass. And when last there, I learned that the grass along the side has been dying from the exhaust fumes and the cows that used to graze right up to the road's edge have been moved away. In actual fact, neither that area nor any other part of Switzerland has pollution that comes even close to our own. But the principle is just as bad. It reminds us that man's reasonable first steps often contain the seeds of troublesome and eventually disastrous trends. After he had altered nature with a dirt road and a horse-drawn carriage, he made it temporarily more enjoyable with a smoother road and a comfortable automobile. But then he went on and on until pleasure was turned into destruction.

Even tourism, bringing so many people from distant lands with bacteria that are far more dangerous when transplanted to new environments, has been turned from pleasure into a form of pollution. There are many known instances of hepatitis having been carried thousands of miles in a matter of hours by one infected person. Even deadlier African or Asian diseases have been barely suppressed before striking Americans or Europeans who had never built up immunity to them. Immunologists do not at all rule out the chance of a sudden plague that might decimate the population. So here is another example of a good thing that threatens to exceed what nature will tolerate: tourists becoming so numerous and so motley as to seem like hordes, rather than guests.

In the face of such problems, the nations of the Atlantic do talk of "co-operating to protect the environment." But they are using only hollow rhetoric. Because the only action that would fit such a phrase would be to order a reversal of developments that have already gone much too far, a cutback in the number of vehicles, travelers, and industrial production. That is clearly impossible under the terms of any government's mandate. No leader feels that "protecting the environment" warrants going to such lengths. And so instead governments urge engines that burn less fuel, fuels that emit less fumes, and exhaust pipes that filter these fumes. These are ways of delaying a climax, not averting it. The mentality exactly corresponds to every other governmental approach in our time. The leaders of all modern countries are now locked into a system so full of conflicting value judgments that they can only pretend to be taking action. What they herald as a great forward movement is usually no more than a lateral wiggle.

America may still have the capacity to survive such behavior for decades to come. Europe is more vulnerable. A crisis—either economic or ecological—would strike there first and harder. So there are Europeans who hope that their altered and diminished relationship with the US will lessen the trend toward American-style mass production and superurbanization. But as most of these same persons lose no opportunity to buy another car or build another factory, the notion that this trend is controlled by America is less than a half-truth.

16

Resisting Americanization

Europe has gone through several phases in its unique relationship with the US. Just since World War II this has included one period of feeling utterly inferior and dependent, a time of striving to emulate some of the US accomplishments, some years of disillusionment, and more recently a reluctant adversary relationship.

This is more of a problem than it might seem, because there is a great fallacy in any attempt by Europe to pattern itself on the US. Europe cannot be at all like America without suffering much more of the unpleasant side effects of affluence—probably to the point of making that affluence counterproductive. America has been able to get away with trying to have a more or less classless society because the vastness of this continent has dissipated effects that would have been unsustainable in a concentrated area.

Europe is essentially a class society to this day. There are few persons who admit this openly or who even see it; but the fact is that vast numbers of Europeans do not at all view themselves as potential presidents or captains of industry. They recognize a definite distinction between "us" and "them" when they think of the rich or the highly educated or the wellborn. This is not because of a great philosophical difference between the peoples, for most Americans are, after all, basically Europeans. It is partly because structure and discipline is somewhat more essential within tight confines. But it is even more directly due to the fact that trying to give all the advantages of what the twentieth century calls a high living standard to millions of people is literally ruinous to any normal-sized environment. Perhaps it can be done *only* in the USA. Other countries can flatten all the classes into one; but then the living standard of this mass must be strictly limited. Even Russia, with its vastness, may not be rich enough in climate and resources to achieve more. And it was, in fact, a Russian who recently admitted at an international meeting, "After all, the world can afford only one United States of America. If there were more countries like you, the planet would suffocate."

Up to now it has been unthinkable to say outright that a society which promises everything to everybody simply will not work, that mental aspirations are subordinate to natural laws. But every hard truth has to be faced at some point, and this one is going to be upon us as a publicly admitted reality before the 1970's are over. Today it is said merely that pollution must be controlled or energy must be conserved. But after a bit it will be admitted that the more realistic way of phrasing this is to say that most people will have to have less.

Still, the fact remains that America's very existence goads Europe to be satisfied with nothing less. Unlike the early 1900's, when Europeans thought of coming to the New World because its streets were paved with gold, they now believe that their own streets should be like ours. They are, but in a very unfavorable sense. They know by now that

America's wealth has also brought mighty problems, but they cannot help feeling that it is demeaning to be second in affluence.

The shifting attitudes and comments of one European manager—an Italian executive who is quite characteristic—will help to demonstrate the evolution of thinking among thousands of others like him:

When we first met in the early 1960's this man was fascinated by any idea that emanated from America. Two years later, he voiced even greater admiration for the remarkable efficiency that seemed to be the birthright of almost any American. "When I was running an operation in Southern Italy I had a very good secretary from the nearby region," he said. "She did what I told her, and I had no complaints. But when she left, it happened that an American girl came to work for me briefly. It was unbelievable how she organized things. She spent less time at her desk than the other one, but she used her head, did many things on her own initiative, and really caused me and several of my assistants to work much better."

In the mid 1960's this Italian came to America for the first time, and he confessed to some disappointment. "Washington is a sad city," he said of our crime-ridden capital. "New York is exciting, but it is a little disillusioning to see so many great things happening with so little leisure to enjoy them."

A year later, when one of his colleagues took a management post in Canada, he said, "I don't think he will be happy. I respect the US and Canada, but I could never work with North American staff. They have no respect for a manager's authority, and that means he must run twice as hard—to set policies and make his people comply."

By now, this executive doesn't much like working with Italian staff either. Their respectfulness toward a manager has sharply diminished. They have learned a good bit about getting things done in fewer working hours, but he feels that they are not done as well. And his company's much greater emphasis on "maximizing profits," its steady insistence on comparing its operating figures with many other European *and American* firms, gives him that same feeling he had in New York—"great things going on, and no leisure to enjoy them." Most significant of all, he *blames America* for having spread this new way of life to the Old World.

There is no room in any of us for disdain that anyone can be both fascinated and appalled by America's values. Europeans are no more paradoxical in their view of us than are the millions of determinedly democratic American tourists who spend a year's savings to cross the Atlantic and look in awe at palaces built by kings and art created for an aristocracy. A woman guide in Budapest, Hungary, moaned that tourists from all countries want to see "only palaces and the old parts of the city. Nobody cares about the new people's housing or the people's stadium." Even Marxist visitors are bored by the slabs that are now called housing. But it does not seem to make them wonder whether the more interesting things of the past might indicate unsuspected merits.

Europeans, when they think of America, have that same ambivalence in reverse. They know by now that it has woes along with wealth. But the very name is synonymous with worldly success, with comfort, with spending ability. They watched Americans continue to come to Europe and spend heavily during years when the dollar was called weak and the exchange rate should have been prohibitive. And so they are sure that Americans are somehow supplied with that most envied of attributes—an endless reserve of purchasing power.

And all of this leads to the question of whether Europeans will welcome more large American-style (and often American-owned) factories into their areas. There was a time when every EEC country sought such enterprises eagerly. Today, they are still encouraged to come into some of the depressed regions where incomes are below the national average; but even in those locales there are people who question the whole process.

First of all, there is resentment and distrust over the fact that companies managed in the American manner are more ready than foreign firms are to let workers go whenever business slows down. Europeans are not quite so paternalistic as Japanese companies, which hold on to full work forces right through severe recessions. But even in Europe, a factory owner feels responsible for the security and future of each worker. Not even the extensive unemployment benefits, now common throughout Europe, that entrust much of this responsibility to the state has ended the custom. And parts of the French civil service have similar lifetime provisions. A Frenchman who succeeds in joining the elite corps of *inspecteurs des finances*, for example, always has a place there, even if he should choose to go and work elsewhere for a time. Whenever he finds that he will be out of other work, he need only write to a central office in Paris and announce that he will be back on its payroll as of a certain date. That office "spreads the net" as its expression goes, and he is neatly caught in it—at whatever grade he had reached before leaving. To such societies, it came as a great shock that some American companies set up plants in Europe or bought up controlling interests in existing ones, then thought nothing of paring the payrolls or even closing down the operation if it seemed wise to its accountants and managers.

· An American plastics manufacturer that bought a British firm reorganized it three times in four years, then sold it to a German company. Each change involved numerous firings and job shifts, some of which led to wildcat strikes by the local unions and aggravated the call from US headquarters for still more changes.

• A US maker of electrical controlling equipment started a plant in southern France and attracted many local people away from their old jobs by offering higher wages. Within six months it decided that a different kind of production line would be preferable, added new machinery, and laid off dozens of employees.

For a time, such happenings actually made it hard for other US firms coming in to hire locals at any wage. They preferred their secure relationships with lower incomes. As American firms were counseled by the US Commerce Department and by foreign governments to avoid such incidents, the best-managed of them worked to overcome the bad feeling. A great many US subsidiaries abroad try to play down their place of origin, trying to appear as locals—sometimes even giving their subsidiaries a name that sounds indigenous. But while there has been a definite improvement in community relations, the belief that working for Americans is far from idyllic does persist.

Second, frivolous as it may sound, this issue of whether to have more US-style factories in Europe often becomes entangled with the subject of food and dining habits. Not just this or that edible product, but the whole matter of mealtimes as high points of each day. It achieves political significance because it so often starts this train of reasoning in the minds of local people whose wishes count with the mayor, the town councilmen, and ultimately with the central government: "Such a factory will create far more jobs in this area. More money around town . . . good for our businesses and property values. Some of the jobs will be for women. That will make it harder to hire a maid or a cook. And the first thing you know, we'll be eating smaller meals, even prepared foods." Or the laboring man might also realize, "More jobs for women means that *my* wife may go to work there. A nice thing—to have an extra income, so maybe we can buy a better car, an electric refrigerator, many things. . . . But then what kind of meals will I have? Maybe even those terrible canned soups instead of a fine *potage* made the same day! Is that progress?"

Already there has been an important shift in the midday habits of Europeans. As cities have grown larger and workers live farther out in suburban areas, it becomes inconvenient or impossible to go home for a major meal and a rest. So more workers ask for a short lunch hour, preferring to eat sandwiches in the park and then end the work day as early as possible. But it is not really a popular arrangement—especially not in southern Europe. And to the extent that it is thought to result from US influence, it gains no friends for America.

Some of this, of course, is unfairly dubbed "Americanization" only because America now has some of the largest factories. Since the industrial revolution actually began in England and the hunger for the jobs and products that it creates is universal, the US is being branded simply because it happened to succeed at something that everyone was trying equally to accomplish. The real question should be whether to resist further *industrialization.* Rationally, that is just what Europe should do. For although it has some pockets of poverty and unemployment, it is dotted much more extensively with overemployment and with the need to import workers from other areas. This is creating a serious problem of ill-treated and disillusioned migrant workers. Physically, their wretched conditions blight the nations they have temporarily adopted; and spiritually, it is a blot on the host nation to find itself so inhospitable to people who come in good faith to do a job. The whole thing dramatizes how little Europe needs more industry. Any government that really cared for its people would say: our cities are already too crowded, our production more than enough to provide jobs for our own population. More factories requiring the importation of foreign workers can benefit only a few entrepreneurs and labor leaders. At this point we must end the process of designing tax laws and other incentives in ways that encourage industrial expansion. Instead, our new rulings will *dis*courage expansion. Without any dictatorial decrees, we will simply make the tax burden much heavier for those who contribute to our problems by creating new plants and new jobs.

Governments, however, are more responsive to the pressure of big capital and big labor than the grumbling of unorganized individuals. So nothing will be done to veer *directly* away from "Americanization." The most that can be hoped for is a little less desperation about keeping the growth rate high, an inclination to let natural forces slow the headlong rush.

Once, when the franc's value had soared abnormally high, I asked a Swiss diplomat whether that might not hurt business in his country—slowing both export sales and tourism. "I hope it does!" he said emphatically. "Of course, the National Council back home would order my execution if they heard me say that. But really, the country would be so much better off if things cooled down a little."

17

Will the EEC Live or Die?

New nations are usually born amid auguries of perpetual futures. "From 1815 to 1965, no less than twenty-seven eternal and sovereign states were born in Europe. During the same period twenty-three eternal and sovereign states disappeared, some of them to be born and die a second time," wrote Louis C. D. Joos in a European Community publication. "Over the past 150 years, a European state has been born or has died on average every three years." And these figures exclude all the German princely states that existed in central Europe during the nineteenth century.

So it is not impertinent to inquire whether a European Community that has not yet made any claim to sovereignty or eternality will eventually go the way of Massa-Carrara, Lucca, Montenegro, or Ukraine. But it is important to note that those and most of the other deceased states of Europe died by being absorbed into larger entities. The tendency, up to a point, does favor synthesis.

In today's European Community there are signs both of health and disease. This is true of most living organisms, the ultimate question of survival depending on whether it has the quality that doctors call "homeostasis"—the ability of a body to react against extremes and keep itself in balance. And the capacity to overcome serious ills *has* been a characteristic of the EEC from the start. In the midst of the Community's worst crises—even during those after-midnight sessions when France was threatening a final break—most close observers felt confident that a compromise would come. But this sense of inevitability, to be valid, must spring from real factors that give symmetry to each problem and furnish the ingredients for compromise.

Does the EEC still have this kind of make-up in the business and material sense? Does it have the elements of unity in its political and psychological life?

From a business standpoint, Germany, the great dynamo that first gave power to the EEC, sometimes seems to be too energetic for the rest of the Community. As Germany went into its "economic miracle" even before the Common Market began, it not only created job opportunities that drew workers in from neighbor countries. It also sent German-made products out to the rest of the world at a record rate, because Germany's people had the old-fashioned habit of not demanding much for themselves. When a country exports far more goods than it imports, its workers are making a sacrifice—letting a large part of the goods they produce go abroad to be enjoyed by others. In return, the nation gets money which it can invest to make itself even more productive and powerful. This used to be considered a very wholesome trait; but today it is an embarrassing one. A neighborhood full of profligates is uncomfortable when one family in the block is hard working and thrifty.

Over and over again, economic crises in the West have featured discussion of "the German problem," and politicians have asked, "What are we going to do about Germany?" The Germans—somewhat dazed—have altered their habits a little. By letting the German mark go up and up in value, they have tried to curb their export sales and to bring in more goods from abroad. But a country, its people, its location, and its resources are fundamental things, not readily changeable by government stratagems. The fear of fuel limitations makes many analysts believe that Germany's trade surpluses will finally be curbed; because German production is largely of a kind that requires heavy inputs of energy, and most of this must be bought from the outside at prices that now are staggering. It will jar the steady ascent of German growth figures, and it has already resulted in layoffs for many migrant workers there. But some of the slowdown was desirable anyway, to dampen the inflationary forces. There is no reason to doubt that the German penchant for hard work and good organization will overcome even the fuel problem relatively better than most neighbor countries.

In trade with the EEC nations, Germany will go on selling more than she buys. Her industry will go on producing much more than the German people themselves consume. And this will give her power which will make some future German politician less amiable and more headstrong than those of recent years have been. Or—if the surrounding countries try to insist on rules that stifle Germany's productiveness—this will create even more danger of a bad reaction within Germany.

The great dilemma of Europe's leaders is how to go on with the principles of free trade and free flow of money which they have all made into a religion, when in fact they don't trust in them at all. They cannot because they have an even stronger belief in high employment and prosperity. The free flow of goods and capital inevitably brings more jobs and wealth to some places than to others. Therefore, governments must keep trying to interfere with the flow just enough to moderate both the good and bad effect. The objective is good, but it requires more delicate adjustment techniques than any that are available today. And even the adjustments themselves tend to boomerang.

Suppose Italy finds its prosperity slowing down and unemployment beginning to creep up. One of the commonest techniques for dealing with this in our era is for the government to make money more plentiful and cheaper. There is a long-held theory that when interest rates are lower businesses tend to borrow more and expand their operations, thereby creating more jobs. It works only feebly, if at all, because when a group of businessmen sit in a committee room and discuss whether to expand the factory, their main concern is with whether they can really sell more goods. If they are optimistic on that score, a somewhat higher interest rate will seldom stop them from borrowing the money to go ahead. Ask any businessman and he will confirm that to you. But if the sales prospects are unexciting, no lowering of the interest rate will lead that committee to build more factories and buy new machinery. So the tampering with interest rates has relatively little effect on the solid side of business. But it does cause money to move in a speculative way—and in the wrong direction. Wise Italians will see that they can earn more interest on their money in some other country. Moreover, they will expect the easy-money policy to cause inflation and erode the value of the lira. Both these thoughts will make money flee from Italy to the very places that need it the least. At some point, government controls usually have to be imposed to stop the unhealthy flow. So all the pious preaching about freedom of money is only lip service as long as conditions are as unequal as they are within the EEC.

And the business differences among the member nations of the Community are, indeed, deeply ingrained. Louis XIV is very much alive today in France's government-business relationship. The Sun King, who made his Versailles bedchamber the geometric center of roads leading outward to all of France, established a pattern of centralized control that persists today. So Paris can direct the course of French business by manipulating the national budget, while similar moves in Germany or Italy have little effect. Any suggested formula for speeding or slowing the economies of the member countries may work well for France and not at all for countries whose regional organization still is somewhat like a collection of principalities.

None of this proves that what Europe has been trying to do is wrong or that it cannot possibly work in the end. It does show that the hopes have been much too great, the pace too rapid. It means that, on the business side, nature will continue to impose its wise limitations on any attempt to change things too fast.

The political outlook has at least as many reasons for skepticism. Bear in mind that the great period of progress toward finding solutions for massive problems came when the US was actively urging European unity and—more important—Russia was actively fueling it with threats. What will happen in a period when neither of these outside forces is acting in that way and the EEC inwardly is beset by labor problems, inflation, and a serious business slowdown?

Might the Common Market actually break apart in the 1970's, I asked a senior State Department planner in Washington. "Yes. I don't expect it, but it cannot be ruled out," he admitted. "Any one of several courses might lead to that kind of result. For instance, a military coup could put one member country on a more nationalistic footing. That could lead to bickering in the Council of Ministers and a series of separatist moves in the other capitals. Or—even more likely—inflation could lead to business failures and a fight for markets. If a few of these countries began trying to block free trade among themselves, ill will would spread fast."

Here the line between politics and business becomes very narrow. It is a *political* necessity for each country to maintain high employment. If that has led to some very bizarre official behavior in the past prosperous years, might it not—in leaner years—precipitate rash acts that now seem unthinkable? If conditions became markedly worse in one nation than another, a government that couldn't provide full employment would at the very least be expected to show evidence of fighting hard to protect jobs. So measures that add up to trade war—exaggerated as they sound at this moment—could become standard behavior among the capitals of Europe. Assuming something short of such economic dislocation, it is more likely that Europe will come to a stretch of dawdling years when its stated aims are neither fulfilled nor abandoned. As EEC Commissioner Ralf Dahrendorf told me, "We are running into many issues of an order of magnitude that we do not have the instruments to cope with." He meant this to indicate that the instruments would be developed. But it seems unlikely that this can be done in short order. More probably, there will be times when the nine nations will only stand and stare at the issues, hardly knowing how to tackle them.

The underlying political drives of the various member countries are certainly not a unifying factor: the small nations are firmly in favor of political integration. Italy leans in their direction, but not enough to force the issue. The largest members are basically opposed to unity. Germany is unsure about actually melting into the West at the cost of separating herself from so many Germanic peoples to the East. France is resolutely dedicated to her own greatness, and therefore willing to play only if she captains the team. And Britain is still made up of island people who are not totally sold even on the commercial aspects of membership; they might agree to remain *partners,* but not to be *part* of the continent.

Those who hope that Europe will coalesce despite these dissenting views are really counting on country after country to be eased into a new attitude almost without realizing it. They expect that 250 million people, who would surely vote a resounding "no" to full European unity if a referendum were held today, will be wheedled along with jobs and benefits and other such political inducements, taken from point to point by the persuasion of their leaders, until finally they find themselves firmly locked in a new nation without knowing quite how they got there. Better than a divided Europe, often on the brink of war? Better than a group of little countries that are helpless in the face of America and Russia? Maybe so. But let no one call it the very model of democracy at work, for it has little to do with the will of the people.

"We are not reaching the people of Europe," one very high EEC official admitted sadly to me. "They don't know what goes on in Brussels or even what the EEC stands for. They understand something of the trade implications, but nothing more. And mainly they don't care."

"Imagine trying to get a large radio or TV audience to watch a speech about the Common Market," scoffs a Dutch politician. "The politics of the EEC is neither understood nor cared about. If the President of the EEC resigns and the whole Commission is replaced, not one per cent of Europeans would recognize the names of the old officials or the new ones."

"Business companies follow the EEC rules and changes, but nobody else does," says a French journalist. "It is still just an economic union, as far as the people of Europe are concerned. Nothing more."

Still, the practical question is whether the general plan

to entice these unknowing people into a new citizenship will work. In order to do so, a great many moving parts will have to keep running just so. Sometimes the nations seem like nine race cars all taking a sharp turn together at high speed. If one of them veers a bit too far and they all begin to correct their positions, the danger of a whole series of collisions is obviously great. The chance, for example, that a business downturn in some member country would be blamed on the EEC by an ambitious politician even raises the possibility that one nation would drop out. It is hard to imagine that such an unprecedented move would fail to generate radical actions on the part of the other eight.

Nor does an even longer look ahead make the prospect for unification brighter. The effect of time is the most complex wild card in the poker game of world politics. For the moment, it is easy to get the impression that the young generation is solidly for European unity and apathetic toward Atlantic co-operation. But there is really no such thing as a generation gap, for babies are born day-by-day and not at twenty-five-year intervals. The thoughts of those who are just a year or two apart become more and more alike as they grow up. And all of them tend, at some point, to relive the emotions of their fathers. So the untried European youth who today see no reason for the existence of NATO are at least passively in favor of European unification, because young Germans and Frenchmen have no remembered reason for hating each other. But if there were a scarcity of jobs or food, parents or grandparents who had lived through past conflicts would be the least likely to find war a thinkable solution. Meanwhile, the youngest persons might be the most ready to use force on each other—and probably even to vie for American help.

Since the young are the Europe of tomorrow, their inclinations have to be given the most weight by a forecaster. And that makes it far from certain that Europeans of coming decades, since they do not know the past, can be counted on not to repeat it.

Adding up the plusses and minuses, it is hard to avoid a conclusion that the EEC has less than a fifty per cent chance of achieving real unity in the next few years—or even in the next several decades. My own working assumption is that Europe in the 1980's will still be a somewhat disjointed Common Market, still a major economic force in the world, but by no means a separate superpower. This is not meant to be a gloomy view. For it is not at all apparent that another superpower is what the world needs. That kind of Europe could very well engage in balance-of-power tactics that would lead to world-wide conflict. A Europe that keeps tying an occasional knot in its frayed ropes and going on may, in the end, prove more durable. As experienced diplomats have found, "It is only the temporary that lasts."

18

Will Atlantic Trade Flourish or Flounder?

The term "détente" is a fighting word. Just as "truce" implies the existence of war, détente or relaxation indicates a very serious degree of tension. It used to be reserved for Cold-War rivals. So it is shocking to find that it has lately crept into discussions of America and Europe.

When France's François-Xavier Ortoli took office as President of the EEC he spoke of "the will to achieve a détente in trade relations." It was no exaggeration of how serious things are. The US and the European Community have actually been near the brink of business war for a number of years. The monetary confrontations and the desperate need on both sides of the ocean to maintain high employment have tempted each government to do whatever was needful in order to win as many trade skirmishes as possible. Talks have kept going and last-minute accommodations have been made only because neither side has dared to face the internal consequences of an all-out business conflict.

Europe has tended to back down more than the US—to an extent that is roughly proportional to Europe's greater reliance on foreign trade. A showdown with America would ensure heavy loss of export sales, and joblessness—thus making the conflict pointless. America would be less damaged by sales loss. But it would suffer the pain of seeing its huge investment in Europe jeopardized. And it might see Europe turn entirely away from America and become a neutral—the greatest foreign policy disaster of modern times. And so trade war, like nuclear war, has been staved off only by a balance of terror.

But deterrence by fear, in this field as in any other, is an unpleasant, and perhaps unreliable, means of maintaining peace. The unthinkable does sometimes come about. A tide of events may push one or more governments into actions that provoke strong responses by others. A sudden veer away from free trade, several protectionist rulings, a slamming of free-trade doors, and reprisals by each nation against the direct investments of others—these are distinct possibilities. Whether the Atlantic allies will turn on to this slippery toboggan or stay clear of it will be decided within the next few years.

A great new round of trade negotiations is now under way. Much depends on the outcome. If they can be brought to heartening conclusions—an announcement of reduced tariffs and other barriers among the Free World countries—the significance will be much greater than the mere increase in trade. It will be a sign that there is enough health in each of the participating nations and governments to make accommodations possible. Only when countries become too weak to compromise must they become enemies. The trade negotiators themselves do not determine these things. They meet in Geneva and discuss the numerical details of tariff rates on various products, always acting on instructions from home. "In actual practice, the men who represent their countries at trade negotiations nearly always want to reach an agreement," a veteran of such talks told me. "These bargaining rounds drag on for several years, and so they become a major segment of a man's career. To have such a round fall through entirely is a bitter personal defeat for each individual involved. So the inner pressure on them is to conclude an agreement, if at all possible."

But these men are doing the bidding of governments that have much broader problems and objectives in mind. The whole economic and political situation in each country helps to determine what concessions are possible on each category of goods. And if one or more of the major nations is not in a position to make enough tariff concessions at the crucial time, no amount of zeal or bargaining skill on the part of the negotiators will change the result.

So the outcome depends more on the sum total of each nation's circumstances than on Geneva discussions. The global circumstances in which this particular negotiation is being held are especially poor. It is so different from those days a couple of decades ago when most economies in the modern world were looking ahead to more years of inevitable growth. At that time there was still tremendous slack in these main nations:

- Many more people were available to be upgraded into better jobs, made into more important consumers.
- Land was relatively plentiful.
- Many highly advanced industries that had become important in the US had not yet made a place for themselves in Europe.

And so each country had a long program of unfinished expansion ahead of it. This meant that tariff concessions which might hurt the sales of this or that industry could be taken in stride. If a few thousand workers were laid off here or there, places could rather easily be made for them in another line. If one country's export sales to another should be slightly damaged by a tariff cut, it would be more than offset by the irresistible force of expanding business into other markets.

Today, there is no inevitability about business expansion. The economies and the companies within them go on growing because they feel that it is a duty. Laws are made, regulations are changed, new initiatives are tried—anything at all to keep meeting a certain growth rate, for a slackening of that rate has come to mean defeat. The danger that the rate might fall and cause a panic on the part of investors and savers and consumers is frightening enough to keep governments enlarging their economies, even when pollution overshadows profits. It is frightening enough to make companies vote new expansion plans even in periods when they cannot clearly envision where the new customers are to come from. And at such a time, any government will think even more carefully than ever about making a tariff cut that might create a net minus in the employment column. Tariff concessions are always based on the thought: "If this causes a loss of one thousand jobs, the concessions we won in return should give us a gain of twelve hundred jobs." But if this is scrutinized with a more and more demanding attitude, there will be more times when negotiators feel unsure of the trade-off and decide against agreement. This is the kind of *general* background that could make it very hard for present-day negotiations between the US and Europe to succeed.

On top of that, the hazy outlook has been more heavily clouded by the uncertainties that increased fuel costs create. Who can foresee how much a Mercedes or a Volkswagen must cost in some future year, if the energy needed to make it and ship it multiplies in price? Who can say what this unknown figure will do to the relative sales of a large car and a small one in America? Or how the energy equation will affect Boeing's sales of passenger planes to Europe? Since almost every one of the thousands of items in world trade is now veiled more than usual by this added mystery, the decision to cut whole groups of tariffs by a certain percentage becomes an even dizzier guessing game than before. Even if hope of success is not dead, the pace of negotiations will certainly be very much slowed.

Bearing in mind the relationship between the EEC Commission and the Council of Ministers, it is interesting to recall that the Commission first established the European posture by submitting to the Council a set of proposals for an overall approach to the great new trade negotiations. This means that the Commission had an opportunity to apply its own language, its own slight nuances to the approach which it felt should be taken. While the Council will have the right to change these ideas up to the final moment of decision, the mere existence of an EEC blueprint does tend to head the Council in that direction.

The Commission's plan, stated in a background note from Brussels, insists on the EEC's continuing dedication to the liberalization of trade. Just as nations have always maintained that their own intent is peaceful, right up to the moment of going to war, countries these days feel that they must give powerful lip service to the principle of free trade. The EEC Commission speaks of the Community's duty to "live up to the international responsibilities which flow from its economic size and power."

But quite naturally the blueprint, without mentioning any other country by name, uses every possible stratagem to suggest negotiating formulae that would advance the EEC position and oppose the approach taken by the USA. It mentions, for example, the fact that great differences exist between the tariff structures of the developed countries. Some countries apply roughly the same amount of tariff to all products, while others apply very high duties to some products and much lower ones to others. The average level may seem to be the same in the two cases, but the effects on trade are enormously different. For the low tariffs often are on products that are not made in that country anyway and which would therefore come in regardless of duties. The very high tariffs may serve to keep out imported goods entirely. This is very different from simply adding a percentage charge onto goods as they come in. It acts more as a barrier that prevents them from coming in at all. The EEC insists that the formula for negotiating on tariffs should aim at leveling off the differences caused by these peaks and troughs. This means adding still another step to the already complex negotiating procedure. For instead of simply discussing mutual reductions, some countries would be asked to make selective changes, especially deep cuts in the duty rates on highly protected products. And of course when the EEC speaks of countries that have such widely varying peaks and troughs, it is referring especially to the USA.

"The formula for lowering tariffs should therefore be based on the principle of the higher the tariff, the greater the reduction in customs duty," says the EEC. This is like suggesting progressive income tax to a nation of rich men. It means that instead of having roughly equal reductions on both sides, the US might be asked to make cuts substantially greater than the ones that would be granted by the EEC. Certain industries that had been allowed to base their entire structure on a high level of protection against imports would be subjected to a sudden and greater adjustment than other lines. Even if American diplomats and negotiators see some logic and equity in this, it will be very difficult to make Congress and the business community agree—especially in a period when the American international trade prospect is far from rosy.

Another major problem area is the reduction of nontariff barriers. These are the various trick devices that nations use to reduce the quantity of incoming competitive goods. They are not simply tariff charges. There are hundreds of stratagems—such as health regulations, special taxes on the size of automobiles, their weight or horsepower, labeling and packaging requirements, inspection procedures that cause incoming goods to stand in warehouses for months, and so on. These are a particularly hard type of trade barrier on which to negotiate, since many countries do not even acknowledge that they exist, and even the admitted ones are often intangible or vague in their effect. France, for example, does not admit that her inspection rules for incoming drug items are intended to keep out foreign products; the fact that she has so few inspectors and the incoming goods somehow wait months to be checked is simply ascribed to an unfortunate shortage of personnel trained in that line. The US does not admit that its bizarre method of computing tariffs on certain foreign chemicals is really a protectionist device, or that duties on incoming foreign whiskey amount to a heavy tax on the water content. Yet experienced international traders know that virtually every country has a screen of gimmickry that hampers, frustrates, and sometimes completely halts the inflow of certain products.

Now, to the old problem of trying to reach mutual bargains on such elusive types of barriers, is added the fact that the US will be negotiating with a group of countries and yet trying to discuss barriers which only individual governments have and control. In other words, the EEC as a group has few nontariff barriers. It does have a general tariff level, and it can negotiate on this in an arithmetical way. But when it comes to the nontariff barriers, the US must take exception point by point to this Dutch rule or that French one. And in many cases, each of the countries has its own separate ways of blocking the importation of a particular product.

As we have seen earlier, the EEC is also insisting on much greater preference for the importation of goods from the less-developed countries. Among other things, it feels that the US should lower its tariffs on products from the backward nations. This "sharing of the burden" is, of course, another of those instances where each country makes an apparently idealistic proposal for a very self-serving reason. It is like the large families in a community asking that even the childless couples share the burden of giving all children a higher education. There may be eventual advantage for all in the general uplift of the community, but it is not the kind of burden sharing that evokes quick enthusiasm.

Meanwhile, the US has its own brand of one-upmanship for the negotiations. It centers on the concept of "linkage," which was devised by former Commerce Secretary Peter G. Peterson. A tough-minded business executive at heart, Peterson believes almost religiously in free trade; but he deplores those past occasions when the US has let other global considerations erode its commercial position. And so, while he was President Nixon's aide on foreign-trade matters, he completely converted that administration to the idea of bargaining with the rest of the world as though our very lives depended on profitable trade.

It is this kind of Uncle Sam—no longer the wealthy philanthropist, but the trader of old—who confronts the Europeans now with the demand for linkage. It means tying the issues of defense costs, monetary problems, and energy shortage to every step of the trade negotiations. "What good is it to set up a certain trade situation if one party or the other can't afford it or can't finance it or can't do it while maintaining a certain level of troop expenditure?" asks a White House expert. "We have to look at all aspects of European and Japanese policy—including their attempts to cut our advantage on high-technology products, for example—and then see how the whole thing balances out."

Among other things, the US—for the first time in memory—is asking for more favors than it is prepared to give in return. It feels that no other arrangement can possibly lead to a solution of the dollar problem. That means the US idea of "how the whole thing balances out" could be a very embarrassing one to the politicians of Europe and Japan, who cannot afford to admit at home that they have given unilateral concessions to wealthy America.

Japan's presence and pivotal role in these negotiations will be yet another negative influence to overcome. It will be recalled that Europeans are terrified of Japanese competition. One of America's demands will be for Europe to reduce its anti-Japanese trade barriers and absorb more goods from Japan. For if refused access to that alternate market, the Japanese have little choice but to keep trying to flood America with their products. Failing that, they might even turn away from peaceful world competition and try again for domination of the Pacific. Europe regards this argument as a roundabout American plea for help in our self-appointed role as policeman of the Pacific. And so they will give in only partially, reluctantly, and in return for considerable concessions from both the US and Japan.

These are just a few of the trade problems that will be standing between America and Europe for some time to come. Issues like them have been compromised in earlier negotiations. But, as said at the beginning of this book, the last time such problems were apparently resolved—in the Kennedy Round of tariff cuts—the agreement was not realistic and the US had to renege on many of its promises. Now the economic climate makes it even harder to agree on anything that would be sustainable. To force a deal at the cost of considerable sacrifices by several of the negotiating nations would be pointless if it clashed with political realities within those nations. Germany, for example, has so often revalued the mark upward, which is an even greater trade concession than cutting tariffs, that its government might find it impossible to go along with major new concessions of a group type.

The prospects for meaningful agreement are not good. Men on both sides are still saying statesmanlike things. Joseph A. Greenwald, US ambassador to the EEC, for example, has said the major industrialized powers should be "ready to reconstruct their trade and monetary systems in the light of changed circumstances but continuing common interests. Everyone now accepts, at least intellectually, that things have changed," says Greenwald, "particularly with respect to the US and the dollar. On the other hand, our common goals have not changed—only perhaps been lost sight of in the day-to-day conflicts, crises, and carping."

Italy's ambassador, Egidio Ortona, says: "The mutual interests we share so greatly eclipse our differences that failure to reach an agreement would be really senseless. Yet it is true that every month spent in disputes greatly increases the danger of lasting bitterness. So I hope we will work at getting together not as if it should be done, but as if it *must* be done."

The one thing sure is, as the Federal Reserve Bank of Chicago has observed, that "there will be no unaffected bystanders. . . . The enlarged Community has the potential to more [*sic*] strongly press its economic will on others and to resist the economic will of others when goals are in conflict." The combined Gross National Product of the nine EEC countries totals three-quarters of a trillion dollars—about two-thirds that of the US, and three times larger than that of Japan. The population is well over 250 million, with a per capita GNP of about three thousand dollars per year. The EEC's exports are about 28 per cent of the world total. And when an EEC policy is put into effect, it can have powerful results in the US. For example, between 1967, when Europe's Common Agricultural Policy was fully implemented, and 1972, US exports to the EEC of farm goods subject to that policy declined by fifteen per cent. Factors of this kind can have such a telling effect on other countries that the chance of a breakdown in negotiations and even a collapse of co-operation—as disastrous as it will seem to all—could burst upon the world, against everyone's will. And trade war would be second only to all-out war in the hardships it would inflict.

19

Can Europe Be Regained?

The conditions in Europe that made America's Vietnam policy such a calamity for the Atlantic Community are still in force.

Enthusiasm for economic progress is languishing. The impulse to stand together politically is moribund. Fear of Soviet aggression is dormant. What a change to come about in little more than a decade!

In 1963 I wrote, "Rightly or wrongly, progress in material things is the great passion of Europeans in these years. . . . Having stirred to a new touch, Europe is amazed to find herself young and vigorous again. She sees herself mirrored in glass-walled skyscrapers and curved windshields. . . . Expectancy is everywhere. There is so much to aspire to, so much to look forward to."

But a healthy appetite for new objects can become an insatiable craving. For all too many Europeans the happy pursuit of a decade ago has become a wild and mindless chase. The demand for more income that will be almost instantly translated into inflated prices has become a conditioned reflex. There is much talk, but no real thought, about the penalty that must be paid by all for building a world in which the volume of spendable cash overbalances the supply of usable goods, edible food, and breathable air.

It was exciting, in the 1960's, to picture a world waiting to be filled with new things. Now expectancy has turned to clamor. Factory plans that brought visions of new jobs now bring only talk of pollution control. New skyscrapers that stirred excitement and pride when they first appeared have led to crowded skylines, which are dreary. Europeans still keep running to fill more of their green spaces with asphalt and cement, but they speak and think of the spaces that are left as the most desirable areas of all.

And this economic confusion is echoed in a loss of political momentum. Even when Charles de Gaulle had just barred Britain's entry into the EEC, I could confidently forecast in 1963 that the Six would add members and go on to much bigger things. Today, when great things have come to pass, there is *no* hope of an early movement toward the nationhood that had been looked for. Even the strongest proponents of complete unification have admitted to me privately that a close co-operation among separate nations is the most they can realistically expect for a good many years to come. The small nations may press for moves toward political unity and threaten to stall economic actions otherwise, but they will lack the weight to make more than token progress.

So the hard reality is that the continent will be more like Charles de Gaulle's vision of a *Europe des Patries* than like the single European nation that his adversaries wanted. It was De Gaulle who insisted that a "Europe of Fatherlands"—a group of co-operating but totally independent national states—was as far as the Old World should go toward unity. That is what Europe is and will continue to be—a collection of separate nations that work together on many practical aspects of daily life, but not in their most important relationships with the rest of the world. Because there will be no real European foreign policy, there will be no single Europe. More particularly, there will be no one policy for dealing with the superpowers.

Along with the economic and political deterioration, the third great factor in Europe's future is the Soviet Union, which both *wants* and *has the power* to keep the Europeans from unifying. In its drive to accomplish this, it is trying first to woo Germany. This would have been unthinkable in the past. Before World War II German ambition struck terror into Russia, and after the war the US had arranged for that country to be firmly locked within a united Western bloc. Now, in the nuclear age, Russia can feel certain of always being able to contain and control any movement within Germany. With the Soviet missiles able to obliterate a nation of that size within minutes, Moscow can confidently feed German hopes and tempt German ambition.

The specific bribe that Russia holds out to Bonn is the right to be the undisputed No. 1 country in trade with East Europe. What it could not allow the Germans to do with Czechoslovakia alone at an earlier stage, it will feel able to permit on a wider basis and in a way that will not threaten the solidity of the Soviet bloc. This is a far larger plum for Germany than it seems, for the communist nations make up a huge mass of people who will need vast amounts of manufactured goods and who can deliver large quantities of raw materials, components, and low-cost labor in return. To a nation that is seeing its great Western markets becoming sated with products, this is like opening a virgin territory to an explorer. And besides, Germany does not approach this with the idea of exchanging its Western riches for new ones from the East. It is offered the chance to have *both.* The Russians hold out visions of future gain without specifying any political or military price; and the Americans dare not order Germany to make an either-or choice, lest such an ultimatum provoke a rash response from a nation with a history of political extremism.

And so Germany pictures herself as the great bridge between East and West, unique and powerful in a way that differs from her past attempts at glory. And the Soviets see themselves hovering over the Germans, neutralizing them, using their technology to uplift East Europe. No longer a menace to Russia, such a Germany—shot through with neutralist pressures internally—will soften the defenses of the West. *For at some point, when the trade has grown important enough, the USSR will make pointed suggestions about Germany's stand on East-West issues. And these will become more insistent, and Germany will have to make concessions.* Even larger trade considerations in the West and the resistance of conservative elements in the country may hold Germany within the NATO orbit. But strongly as many of that country's leaders feel about the link with America, I cannot imagine that the growing tendency to look both West and East will make her anything but a weakening factor in the EEC, NATO, and the Atlantic Community.

The Soviets will exert similar pressures on other West European countries. And the Netherlands and Denmark—both laden with neutralist sentiment—stand in the greatest danger of being lured away from the alliance. Even without an overt break in the NATO ties, the significant fact is that a combination of debilitating internal forces and subtle Soviet advances will make the West doubt its own cohesion and resolve.

It would be dramatic to say that there will be a new map for Europe—a gray zone of neutralism bulging westward from the iron curtain to the Atlantic at one point. That would overstate the case. Yet the Soviet accomplishment in having undermined the reliability of Europe's core cannot be denied. Only the historic doubtfulness of Russia's own hold on East European allies in time of crisis helps to mitigate it a little.

Deterioration of the Atlantic partnership has reached the point where Europeans and Americans can now actually envision the possibility of going separate ways. This is more than a personal impression on my part. It is in the minds of the leaders. A very thoughtful ambassador from a Common Market country told me: "Once there was a feeling that the US and Europe *must* be the closest of allies—the Atlantic partners against the world, if necessary. Now some Europeans think otherwise. The young generation does the most questioning, of course. But even the men I see in major meetings are swayed by the controversy. And when they relax for a friendly chat, some of them ask whether America and Europe might not consider having a new relationship—like any other two large peoples who are not fighting each other, but not married either." He hastened to add, "I don't feel that way myself, but I agree that the question should be re-examined."

On the American side, Henry Kissinger has very different ideas about Europe than did our Secretaries of State of the 1950's. "Henry holds the future of European unity in the palm of his hand," one of his colleagues told me very recently. It was not said boastfully, but ruefully, because the comment came from a dedicated believer in European integration. He continued, "The Secretary can deal with Europe as a bloc or he can tempt some of the countries to back away from the others. I am not at all sure that he doesn't want to see the EEC fall apart. He is constructing his own mental picture of what kind of world is best for America, and I don't think it includes a united Europe or a closely knit Atlantic Community."

. . .

From this point forward, the course of events seems likely to develop along these lines: the very fact that Germany and some smaller EEC nations incline toward neutralism will make others fearful and nostalgic for friendship with America. Which others they will be is quite predictable. Washington will have a chance to resolidify some of its relationships with traditional allies in Europe. The most openly pro-American will be Britain, Belgium, and Italy. The "special relationship" that has linked us with the UK will be kept as warm as ever in this new Europe. Italy, which departed only during the Mussolini years from a historic friendship with this country, may well fall into a new form of government; but it will need a rich and powerful friend, and will value its ties to America more than any other.

Then there is France. Most US officials privately assume that French policy will continue to be essentially anti-American, however different Giscard d'Estaing's style may be from that of his predecessors. And it is perfectly true that the pursuit of national goals by a country that is so dedicated to its own identity will often add up to courses of action that make difficulties for the US. But that is not as bad as the harassed men of the State Department imagine. For the positions that Paris has taken on gold, money, trade, relations with the communist world, and other issues have usually deserved more respect than Washington has accorded them. A troublesome nation is not necessarily a poor ally in time of real need. France, for example, will not formally rejoin NATO; but she will increasingly co-operate in the logistical arrangements that are vital to NATO's real worth.

Steering her own course, France will be independent-minded, but not at all neutral. For one thing, the sight of Germany becoming less predictable will maintain France's underlying interest in US ties. But apart from that, no nation of Europe is firmer in its determination to avoid Moscow domination. France has made some serious policy mistakes, especially the 1954 refusal to join a European defense plan—which forced Germany unwillingly to form a separate national army. But most French judgments in recent decades have been acute. And no foreseeable government in Paris would give Soviet considerations equal weight with American ones.

When it comes to the peripheral nations of Europe, there are at least three firm and three problematical areas. The northern countries are relatively predictable. Norway, for example, is a staunch NATO member that asks only to be allowed a voice in Atlantic affairs and the right to abstain from the frantic industrial development and urbanization of other Western nations. Sweden and Switzerland will cling to their neutrality and will not hesitate to speak out against Washington on an occasional issue; but there is no question of their preference for the American system over the Soviet one, and therefore no cause to fear a worsening of relations.

But three southern nations have questionable futures. Geographically and logically, Spain, Portugal, and Greece have far more to gain from a pro-Washington orientation than from neutrality or a leftward lean. But Portugal's well-organized communist party and its band of radical young military officers make the chance of an irrational policy veer loom large. Spain's potential power struggle after so many years of one-man rule could also lead it into uncharted policy paths. And Greece's turn away from America and NATO after her big Cyprus setback of 1974 will leave strains in the relationship for a long time to come.

In the Greek case, however, we see an instance of how useful France's individualism can be. For the French ambition to become a mini-superpower in the Mediterranean can help to balk Soviet efforts to lure Greece—and perhaps other small nations of that area—into Moscow's orbit. When Greece became disillusioned with the US, it did not have to turn to Moscow as its only alternative supporter. It could form ties with France, instead, rely more on French military equipment, and still stay within the Free World framework. So the hierarchy of second-level nations that act as intercessors and supporters for even smaller countries can help America to have tolerable situations even where it does not dominate.

But at best, it has to be recognized that this will result in a less satisfactory Europe than we have known in the last quarter-century. The new alignments—subtle and unannounced, in fact often denied—will create stresses in many of the practical aspects of both European and Atlantic life. The Common Market nations will go on trading more among themselves than with the outside world, but customs procedures at the various European borders will not be phased out anywhere near as rapidly as had been hoped. Exceptions to the rule of complete free trade will remain numerous. Monetary co-operation will be repeatedly heralded, as one new device follows another; but each attempt will break down after a time, and the goal of monetary union will not be reached in the foreseeable future. American investments in Europe will slow their climb. But here again, generalization is inappropriate. Investment in England will eventually thrive. In the Netherlands it will stall. Some countries that have predictable governments will attract US investors and traders. Others will move capriciously and frighten off the businessman.

Unappealing as it may be to go back to thinking of the Old World in this fragmentary way, after years of calling it just "Europe," it is necessary and realistic. Europe will not abandon the Common Market; some of its programs and projects will even be enlarged. Many of the West's ties will survive the most difficult strains. But strains there will be, and old-fashioned balance of power there will be. And one of the greatest questions confronting American foreign policy is how the US will deal with the situation as it is.

The blunt fact is that forces tending to pull apart both Europe and the Atlantic partnership are growing stronger than those that hold it together. If left unopposed, they will prevail. The destructive changes they have already worked leave no doubt of that.

Recall that the Atlantic arch once was beginning to be much more than a mere alliance. In 1963 Britain's ambassador to the US was pledging that if his country finally joined the EEC, "Our whole influence would be exerted to ensure that Western Europe became an even stronger pillar supporting one side of the arch of the Atlantic Community." There was hope that something akin to trans-Atlantic nationhood was being conceived. But that was before America took Europe's friendship for granted and put it below Southeast Asia on its list of priorities. The judgment that Plutarch directed at Hannibal could have been turned on America: "You know, Hannibal, how to gain a victory, but not how to use it."

Now there is no strong arch—hardly any arch at all—and the pillars at both ends are somewhat altered. America has suffered blows to its self-confidence, to its respect for government, and to its economic structure. Even greater is the change in the European pillar.

In such circumstances, can the zealous spirit of the past be recaptured? Unfortunately not. It had sprung up in the afterglow of a great joint victory. As long as the momentum was kept up, the countries made astonishing sacrifices for the sake of unity. But now that it has been lost, and now that Russia has the wit to mask her menace, I cannot foresee any likely event that might spur a comparable wave of selflessness. Summit meetings and lofty pronouncements may be attempted. But they will be followed by only grudging action. The reasons for making national sacrifices in the interest of unity are simply not visible to the people—and hence not politically practical.

But let us be clear on one thing: Americans and Europeans need each other as much as ever in order to survive in freedom. If they cannot summon the zeal to form a true community, they must at the very least work unceasingly to keep the military alliance invigorated. As Morton A. Kaplan pointed out in a study for Stanford University's Hoover Institute, Europe cannot be a party to a nuclear war without being wiped out. It is not even a genuine continent, but "merely a peninsula on the Eurasian land mass. Our image of armies marching back and forth across the face of Europe leads us to forget that the distance from the East German border to Paris is roughly the width of the state of Pennsylvania. . . . Europe is a toy war ground."

And yet that small area contains much of what we value most in the world. If the US now accepts the principle that it cannot be policeman to the entire globe, neither can we be every country's best friend at one time. Choosing the friendships that count most is one of the most delicate arts of foreign policymaking. Our government made a curious choice in the 1960's, trading a long marriage with Europe for a still-undefined relationship with Southeast Asia. This has put us in greater peril than we realize. But US size, strength, wealth, and magnetic power are still too great to justify despair.

America will not, in the end, allow the European states to become a group of Russian colonies. Apart from the material facts of trade and investment, we will not permit the people with whom we share a common past to lose the character and freedom that are part of our own lives. Nor will we be any more willing in the future than we were twice before in this century to sit in fearful isolation while another power becomes greater and dominates most of the modern world.

Historically, we have always been very slow to recognize this kind of choice when it was before us. It faces us again now. Only by making Atlantic relations first among our foreign priorities can we begin to retrieve the power and the prestige that we lost in the 1960's.

Index